ACCESS & EXCELLENCE

ACCESS & EXCELLENCE

THE
OPEN-DOOR
COLLEGE

John E. Roueche
and
George A. Baker III

Published by The Community College Press, a
division of The American Association of Community
and Junior Colleges, The National Center for
Higher Education, 1 Dupont Circle, N.W., Suite 410,
Washington, D.C. 20036.

ISBN 0-87117-162-7

CONTENTS

DEDICATION

This book is dedicated to Valleau Wilkie, Jr., Executive Vice President of the Sid W. Richardson Foundation, Fort Worth, Texas; to the Board of the Sid W. Richardson Foundation; and to Dr. Robert H. McCabe, President, the Board, administration, faculty, support staff, and students of Miami-Dade Community College who implement well the community college mission of access with excellence.

PREFACE

Acquiring a distinct identity has been a persistent problem which has challenged community colleges over the years. The diverse functions and services community colleges provide tend to blur their image. Further complicating the definition of the role and status of community colleges is their tradition as open-door institutions, a policy which has brought them a cross section of the community with a heavy concentration of students from lower socioeconomic backgrounds and a wider range of cultural origins compared with those of most other colleges. The diversity among community college students is accompanied, for the most part, by academic achievement scores skewed toward the lower levels. From this situation arises a question all too familiar to those who work in community colleges: Can both access and high academic standards be achieved?

We believe we have found convincing evidence to justify an affirmative answer. In searching for a solution to the dilemma posed by the open door, we decided to look at community colleges that successfully meet the needs of their students. Thus, we decided at the outset of our study to examine exemplary rather than normative institutions. Further, for our sample, we needed colleges with concrete outcome data indicative of educational effectiveness. After a selection process to determine our sample, we focused our study on Miami-Dade Community College in Florida, chosen by a national panel of experts according to specific criteria as representative of the best among this country's community colleges.

Our research on Miami-Dade took the form of an in-depth investigation funded by the Sid W. Richardson Foundation, Fort Worth, Texas. The Richardson Foundation has a history of interest in and support of programs for improving the quality of American education; Valleau Wilkie, Executive Vice-President of the Richardson Foundation, invited us to submit a proposal for support of our study. The Richardson grant in April 1984 launched our research of exemplary public schools and community colleges. In the first part of our study, *Profiles in Teaching Excellence: America's Best Schools*, we investigated junior and senior high schools selected as "excellent" by the Department of Education's Secondary School Recognition Program (SSRP) in 1983. The community college investigation comprises the second half of our year-and-a-half-long study of educational excellence in America.

We selected the in-depth case study format for our investigation of the organizational climate, leadership, teaching, systems, programs, and student outcomes at Miami-Dade. A qualitative, descriptive study of a successful institution is probably more valid and presents a more accurate picture of the interrelated components that result in the effective delivery of educational systems to a diverse adult population than any other kind of survey research that could be employed on the same subject. Given a detailed profile and description of an outstanding college, others can replicate and transform the organizational model, the leadership model, the teaching model, and the systems model from this investigation and install them in their own organizations. The models presented in this study are transferable to other community colleges which are also facing the challenge of open access while maintaining high academic standards. Thus, the value of the findings of our study lies in the descriptions of workable solutions to common problems faced by open-door colleges. Further, the findings clearly support the contention that open access can be maintained and excellence achieved at the same time.

Therefore, just as Burton Clark (1960) set out to depict the character of the junior college through institutional analysis, we endeavor to reveal the character of Miami-Dade in our analysis. This college represents an institutional type. It has developed systems, methods, and policies of leadership and teaching which can work in similar institutions. Discussion of each component is meant to reflect the general organizational character of the college. The portrait we present is an attempt to show the organizational whole or the "gestalt" of an institutional type which is applicable to others like it and is worthy of emulation. The study is organized along the following lines:

Chapter I presents the rationale for the study and the Roueche-Baker Community College Excellence Model depicting the character of Miami-Dade.

Chapter II gives a brief history of the college and describes the context surrounding the educational reforms.

Chapter III outlines the reforms initiated, planned, and implemented by the Miami-Dade staff in a collaborative effort.

Chapter IV presents the results and outcomes of the reforms.

Chapters V, VI, and VII present our findings regarding the organizational climate, the leadership, and the teaching at Miami-Dade.

Chapter VIII concludes the portrait of Miami-Dade by summarizing the findings.

In a study as comprehensive as this, it is impossible to acknowledge every individual who significantly contributed to its completion. However, we would like to take this opportunity to thank those without whose help the study would not have been possible.

First, we sincerely appreciate the gracious support of Dr. Robert McCabe, President of Miami-Dade Community College, and his wife, Bonnie. Without their patience and understanding, this study would have been impossible. Dr. McCabe helped field-test and pilot our instruments and assisted our Texas research team in every way possible during our on-site visits to Miami-Dade's four campuses. We would also like to express our gratitude to Ms. Suzanne Skidmore, Assistant to the President, for providing the research team with administrative assistance, answering our numerous requests, and providing us with voluminous documentation. Further, we would like to thank those individuals who made time in their busy schedules during our visit to Miami-Dade to lend special assistance to the research team: Dr. Terrence Kelly, Vice President of North Campus; Dr. Elizabeth Lundgren, Vice President, Medical Center Campus; Dr. William Stokes, Vice President, South Campus; Dr. Maureen Lukenbill, Director of Faculty, Staff and Program Development, South Campus; Dr. Suzanne Richter, Dean of Instruction, Wolfson Campus; Luis Klitin, Director of Educational Technology and Campus Operations, Medical Center Campus; Ms. Marta Quintana, Secretary, Wolfson Campus; Ms. Pat Ballard, Secretary, North Campus; Ms. Barbara Deegan, Secretary, South Campus; and Ms. Jackie Claflin, Secretary, Medical Center Campus.

In addition, our very special thanks go to Dr. John Losak, Dean for Institutional Research, and his staff for conducting the process of selecting exemplary professors and administrators for participation in our study, for administering our climate instrument, and for providing invaluable documentation of institutional research data.

We wish to give special acknowledgement to the outstanding administrators and professors participating in our study who are the heart of our investigation. The names of these outstanding individuals are listed in the text. Thanks to them for their thoughtful responses, for their patience and understanding, and for their enormous contributions to educating and helping adults in our society.

For summarizing the history of Miami-Dade and the research documentation of the reforms, we owe a special debt of gratitude to Ann Parish, herself an outstanding educator in the Austin Independent

School District. Her meticulous attention to detail, her concern for accuracy, and her excellent writing ability are all greatly appreciated.

Patricia L. Mullin and Nancy Hess Omaha Boy served admirably as senior researchers with us on the Richardson study. Each brought to the project many years of teaching experience in both public schools and community colleges. They have made major contributions to the study through their data collection and analysis efforts and their contributions to the final manuscript. Currently, Dr. Omaha Boy is serving as Executive Dean at the branch campus in Omak, Washington, of Wenatchee Community College. Dr. Mullin is Associate Dean of Continuing Education for Fort Steilacoom Community College in Steilacoom, Washington.

Very special thanks go to Libby Lord, a University of Texas staff colleague, for managing the many details involved in producing the manuscript, and to Suanne D. Roueche, director of the National Institute for Staff and Organizational Development (NISOD) for the countless editions of chapters and manuscripts she read and edited. We thank Dolores Payton for her diligent work in word processing the manuscript. We gratefully acknowledge Nanci Bernbrock, who provided expert word processing and excellent editing. Her suggestions added greatly to the quality of the final manuscript. We are most appreciative to Barbara Shapiro for her final editorial services and to Eisenberg Associates for overall publishing coordination of this project.

John E. Roueche
George A. Baker III
Austin, Texas
August 1985

FIGURES

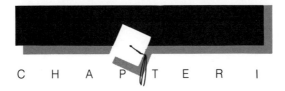
CHALLENGE
OF THE
OPEN DOOR

Give me your tired, your poor,
Your huddled masses yearning to breathe free,
The wretched refuse of your teeming shore,
Send these, the homeless, tempest-tossed, to me:
I lift my lamp beside the golden door.

The New Colossus: Inscription for the Statue of Liberty,
New York Harbor by Emma Lazarus (1849–1887)

In accordance with democratic ideals, every human being should be allowed, if not encouraged, to develop his or her fullest potential. Human development is a continual, lifelong process and is essential to democratic life. Equal opportunity, good citizenship, and economic well-being, all concepts of a free society, depend on a free education for all citizens. Indeed, freedom is only gained and retained through a constant search for knowledge and understanding. Thomas Jefferson, one of the first Americans to advocate free public education, recognized that democracy, in order to flourish and develop, demands an intelligent, well-informed populace.

The need for an enlightened citizenry eventually led the state of Massachusetts to establish common schools in 1837; these schools were the beginning of free education in this country. It was not until 1862, with the Morrill Land Grant Act establishing land-grant colleges, that greater access to higher education was achieved. Thus, the "people's college" was born. Later, in 1896, William Rainey Harper broadened the base of higher education by founding the first junior college at the University of Chicago.

Nearly everyone who has written about the community college alludes to this unique American institution as a democratizing force in higher education. At least one advocate of community colleges has referred to them as "the Ellis Island of higher education" (Vaughan, 1983, p. 9). Although no one expects community colleges to solve all of society's ills, these institutions have been, and continue to be, manifestations of the American dream of equal opportunity for all, regardless of religion, ethnic group, or socioeconomic status.

The eminent educator Alexis Lange has described the basic underlying principle of democracy as the "continuity of educational opportunity" and the "completeness of such opportunity" (1927, p. 93). Furthermore, he saw the junior college as the vehicle for realizing this fundamental democratic precept. The focus of the junior college, according to Lange, is "not on the few [whose rights to an abundance of educational life, liberty, and happiness remain sacred] but the many, whose right to the means of making a life and of making a living are equally sacred" (p. 99). Later, Bogue (1950) and others reiterated these themes.

The community college movement stems directly from further application of the same principle that led to universal elementary and high school opportunities for the masses in this country. With the advent of the community college, the principle of free public education was extended beyond the high school level to the thirteenth and fourteenth grades. Thus, as Bogue (1950) has stated, one critical role of the community college is to ensure the wider diffusion of higher education within our society; consequently, the term "movement" is applied to the community college.

Because community colleges contribute to the continual process of human development and have grown out of the needs of the masses, they have been called "democracy's college," "opportunity college," and like the land-grant colleges, "the people's college." As early as 1936, Hollinshead asserted that the junior college should be a community institution meeting community needs, providing adult education and educational, recreational, and vocational activities, and placing its facilities at the disposal of the community. Therefore, the "open door" to higher education had been well established by 1944, when the numbers of students rose sharply with the passage of the G.I. Bill of Rights, which provided substantial funding for education to veterans of war.

In 1947, the philosophy of open access was further advanced by the Truman Commission on Higher Education, which strongly advocated education for all and established the basic functions of community colleges—providing proper education for all the people of the community without regard to race, sex, religion, color, geographical location, or financial status. Expressing a similar view, Bogue stated in 1950 that education is a never-ending process "of the community, by the community, and for the community" (p. 94).

Further expansion of enrollments in two-year colleges occurred in the 1950s, in part because the land-grant colleges began closing their doors to some high school graduates through the establishment of admission requirements. Later, during the 1960s, the baby boom continued to increase enrollments in all colleges. With this increase in numbers, and the "open-door" policy, came a dramatic increase in student diversity in all two-year colleges.

While the removal of academic, economic, social, and geographical barriers serves to democratize higher education, it also poses a dilemma: the problem of providing open access with quality. Thus, the question has been raised many times over, for nearly three decades, whether community colleges can deliver quality education and at the same time offer open access to those programs. As Cross (1976) has made clear, equal opportunity is not just gaining admission to college: "Educational opportunity means more than the right to meet minimal standards; it means the right to develop one's talents to maximum effectiveness" (p. 3). She describes the access model as successful at increasing the availability of higher education for previously excluded segments of the population but incomplete nevertheless. By itself, the model of open access will not bring about the equal opportunity that it promises unless instruction is improved and curriculum is reshaped.

Consequently, much controversy surrounds the concept of the open-access policy. For example, many view the concept of expanding access as a major contributor to the decline in academic standards. David Riesman, a professor at Harvard University who has written widely on American colleges, makes this point:

> To say there should be universal access to college seems fair. It seems egalitarian, but it's been destructive because students think you don't have to strive in high school. There's the illusion that you can always recover so the whole level has dropped (cited in Feinberg, 1984, p. A6).

Others, including Zwerling (1976), claim the "people's colleges" do not serve the "people." To the contrary, he asserts that the "hidden function" of community colleges is the deliberate channeling of students to their appropriate positions in the social order. Thus, according to Zwerling, the primary function of the community college is to preserve the social status quo, and thereby prevent upward mobility for the lower socioeconomic groups in society. In light of Zwerling's criticism, attrition becomes a major function of the two-year college rather than the problem it is perceived to be by advocates of the community college. To underscore this point Zwerling cites Astin, whose research demonstrates that attending a two-year college—controlling for all other variables such as academic ability, family income, and so on—appears to increase the likelihood of a student's dropping out. The term "cooling out" was coined by Burton Clark (1960), who defined this function as a kindly, systematic process aimed at helping the academically under-prepared student to tone down his aspirations and accept more realistic goals suited to his capabilities. Zwerling sees this process as the school system's effort to deceive and manipulate students, causing them to reach for less than they are capable of accomplishing.

On the other hand, there are many who believe that access and excellence can and do exist simultaneously. "Fortunately, the demand to educate everyone up to the level of his ability and the demand for excellence in education are not incompatible. We must honor both goals. We must seek excellence in a context of concern for all" (from the 1958 Rockefeller Brothers Report, p. 22). The purpose of this book is to describe and offer evidence of how quality and excellence have been and continue to be achieved at an American community college—one that faces problems typical of most community colleges in this nation.

THE PROBLEMS

Open access increases the demand that community colleges respond to the many special needs of the students they admit. Too often, institutions have welcomed new populations of students while failing to serve these students' unique needs. More specifically, a major problem accompanying an open-access policy is the generally low college aptitude found among an unselected student population. This problem is compounded when students, regardless of their college potential, are offered unfettered choices from available programs. Finally, a student body with relatively low academic achievement influences the college and shapes its character; this factor affects how long students stay, how many graduate, and how many transfer to other colleges. Understandably, an unselected student body is characterized by large turnover.

The problems caused by diversity and low academic ability among students force community colleges to assume certain roles. For instance, they often become screening agents for other colleges and universities, a role which affects the image of the college. Consequently, outsiders tend to view the community college as a place for third-rate students, an identity the college is clearly reluctant to embrace. Yet refusal to cope with these dilemmas would be denial of the general democratic belief in equal opportunity for all, the underlying philosophy of the community college that was discussed earlier in this chapter.

Clark (1960) pinpoints a problem stemming from these diverse factors. Many among an unselected student population experience a conflict in values. In accordance with the values of a democratic society, individuals are encouraged to develop to their fullest potential, and attending college is seen as one of the most valid means of achieving this goal. However, some students in open-door colleges are encouraged to set unrealistic goals relative to their academic preparation and ability. They are encouraged by family and friends, i.e., social expectations, to go on to four-year colleges or universities, yet they lack the academic skills to do so. Clark describes the situation as one of "structured failure"; that is, "the disjuncture between ends and means, between the open door and standards, dooms large numbers of students to failure" (p. 162). In response to this problem, Clark suggests that one critical role of the community college is to provide a "cooling out" function for students which results in their acceptance of more realistic personal goals that match their abilities more closely.

Consequently, a basic conflict continues to challenge the open-door college: societal pressure based on democratic ideals for open entry versus concern for quality and high standards. Internal and external societal factors alike pull from both sides of the issue. Social pressure and recent declining enrollments call for open access, whereas colleges and universities, as well as outside groups, want to demand high standards.

Addressing these apparently conflicting demands is complicated by the fact that the community college lacks a distinct organizational identity. Even the community college leadership debates whether the term "college" correctly describes its function. Although the institution is unique in offering both career programs and associate degrees, it also overlaps the work of colleges and universities in its transfer function and the work of technical high schools and trade schools in its occupational/technical function. Furthermore, these areas often overlap within the institution, since many career degrees have some transfer as well as technical courses as degree requirements. As a result, the identity of the community college becomes blurred and problematic. Medsker (1960) describes the reality of the issue: "No unit of American higher education is expected to serve such a diversity of purposes, to provide such a variety of educational instruments, or to distribute students among so many types of educational programs as the junior college" (p. 4).

Although the problem of coping with greater diversity among students has existed since the inception of community colleges, it has never been so prominent as it was during the 1960s when the higher educational system contended with overwhelming numbers of students. Today, the problem of diversity persists, fueled by a distinct change in the composition of students desiring an education beyond the high school. A burgeoning number of students of all ages from diverse countries and cultures are coming to college with learning problems, and with unique socioeconomic problems, such as the challenges facing single parents and women returning to the workplace. The pluralism we find in community colleges today has been unparalleled in the history of the American community college movement.

Bogue, Clark, Medsker, Cohen, and Brawer all identify problems specific to the community college. However, we have limited our focus in this discussion to those most directly related to the open-access-with-quality issue. Thirty-five years ago Bogue presented a comprehensive list of the problems confronting the community college; these problems persist today. Of particular relevance here are problems regarding counseling and guidance. As he asserted, the community college, in order to recognize individual differences among students, needs an organized and well-financed program of student personnel services. He recognized the importance of the time-consuming task of personalized and individualized counseling and guidance, involving accurate diagnostic practices, advisement, placement, and follow-up in conjunction with the instructional staff.

A quarter of a century ago, Medsker (1960) also named at least two criticisms of the community college which persist today: (1) failure to meet some of its claims and (2) failure in some instances to achieve an identity of its own. He identified three areas relating to these criticisms: (1) lack of emphasis on career education, (2) inadequacy of student personnel services, and (3) deficiencies in general education. First, most community colleges do not follow up on their graduates (which we grant is not an easy task), and thus do not have good data about the careers of those graduates or the relationship, if any, between their college experiences and their occupations. Second, adequate counseling and advisement was and is still lacking. Third, a commitment to general education appeared then, and appears now, to be absent, a fact reflected in the low number of integrated course offerings and in the failure to meet objectives of general education within conventional courses.

Despite the problems and criticisms facing the community college, Cohen and Brawer (1982) assert that these institutions must continue to respond with the "cooling out effort," i.e., to assist people in finding jobs, to provide connections, to award credentials, and to provide short-term, ad hoc learning experiences for everyone, even those who do not go on to higher formalized learning. To continue to enhance equal opportunity is important even—perhaps especially—in the face of adversity. As viable educational institutions, community colleges assist individuals to become more effective, responsible members of society and help to provide a means of upward social and economic mobility for individuals of any age.

THE SELECTION PROCESS

While U.S. high schools have the Secondary Schools Recognition Program, no national program recognizes community colleges for institutional efficacy and performance quality. Therefore, we were faced with two problems in our community college study: (1) how to select a small number of colleges for close study, and (2) where to find excellent colleges with evidence of student persistence, retention, and completion rates—uncommon data in community colleges. Thus, we needed to investigate not only excellent institutions but also those which had documented their systems, programs, and outcomes.

In order to select colleges as models for our study of excellence, we began with a cursory search of the literature of the last five years regarding the community college. We consulted the *AACJC Journal, Community College Review, Community College Frontiers, New Directions for Community Colleges,* and various new books since 1978. We were looking for community colleges most cited for emphasis and focus on teaching excellence.

We also assembled a panel of authorities on the community college who had demonstrated particular interest in staff development and teaching effectiveness in their research or in their scholarly writing. Twelve individuals were solicited for their rank order nominations of five community colleges known nationally for success in classroom instruction. The two co-directors of the research project also participated in the nomination process. The following were members of the national Panel of Community College Experts:

Dr. Louis Bender, Florida State University
Dr. Dale Campbell, North Carolina State University
Dr. K. Patricia Cross, Harvard University
Dr. Jim Hammons, University of Arkansas
Dr. Bart Herrscher, University of Houston
Dr. Walter Hunter, University of Missouri
Dr. Terry O'Banion, Executive Director, League for Innovation in Community Colleges
Dr. Richard Richardson, Arizona State University
Dr. Dayton Roberts, Texas Technical University
Dr. Al Smith, University of Florida
Dr. Bob Sullins, Virginia Polytechnical Institute and State University
Dr. Dale Tillery, University of California

(Professors John Roueche and George Baker of The University of Texas at Austin, co-directors of the study, also participated in the nomination process.)

Criteria for nomination were as follows:
1. institutions recognized nationally for their ability to encourage and increase student success,
2. institutions that develop and pursue policies and standards that fully support the concept of the open door while emphasizing quality in instructional and support programs,
3. institutions that enjoy strong and dedicated leadership, especially in the perceived influence of the president in pursuing excellence,
4. institutions that select, evaluate, reward, and develop exceptional teachers in all aspects of the comprehensive mission of community colleges.

First-place nominations received five points and fifth place, one point. Each panel member nominated Miami-Dade Community College as one of his or her five choices. Most important, Miami-Dade was the first choice of twelve of the fourteen panel members. In addition, four other community colleges received multiple nominations from the panel; each of the five colleges selected as outstanding received nominations from at least four panel members. The rank order of the colleges with the points they received is listed below.

Institution	Points
Miami-Dade Community College Miami, Florida	65
Jefferson Community College Louisville, Kentucky	18
Lane Community College Eugene, Oregon	15
De Anza College Cupertino, California	12
Central Piedmont Community College Charlotte, North Carolina	10

Key:
1st Place Nomination = 5 points
5th Place Nomination = 1 point

Clearly, the panel members recognized Miami-Dade as an exemplary institution according to our criteria. Consequently, we decided to abandon our original research protocol of investigating several exemplary colleges and to conduct instead an intensive in-depth case study of Miami-Dade Community College. After talking with President Robert McCabe of Miami-Dade and verifying that student data were available, we decided an intensive investigation of one outstanding community college should yield an excellent model for other institutions to follow.

THE RESEARCH DESIGN

The origin for the design of our study goes back a quarter of a century to Burton Clark's landmark study (1960) of San Jose Junior College in California. Based on Clark's model, our study attempts to delineate the character of a community college selected as exemplary, to show how this character was determined, and to indicate its consequences.

According to Clark, an intensive case analysis is necessary for assessing, systematically and in detail, the nature of an organization. Therefore, our report is based upon qualitative, descriptive research and does not purport to be a normative study. The strength of the case study approach lies in the fact that a number of interrelated activities, rather than a few selected variables, make up institutional performance. Case study research allows for investigation of the many interconnected variables operating in an environment. Surveying a large number of organizations on a few variables or using a single technique for gathering information was an inappropriate method for accomplishing our end—i.e., to present a rich description of the organizational, program, administrative, and instructional characteristics associated with positive outcomes for students in a community college setting.

For the study, we designed and developed four instruments: (1) an open-ended questionnaire to gather self-analyses of professors selected by peers and administrators for teaching excellence, (2) an open-ended questionnaire to gather self-analyses both from second-level administrators (deans, associate deans, and one director) selected by peers and faculty for excellent performance, and from the president and vice presidents, (3) an adapted Likert scale to measure organizational climate, and (4) a Likert-scale questionnaire to measure student responses to professors who were selected for teaching excellence.

Hence, we collected information through observations (conducted during on-site visits), official institutional documentation (especially documents from the institutional research office), and structured interviews of the president, board chairman, first-level administrators, second-level administrators selected for excellent performance, and professors selected for teaching effectiveness. McClelland's Behavioral Event Interview Technique (BEIT, 1978), the coding technique used in the first phase of the study, was employed to analyze the content of both the structured interviews and the open-ended questionnaires.

Our findings clearly indicate that open-door colleges can attain and maintain high standards of achievement, that quality can be achieved if organizations behave in ways that help students learn. The Roueche-Baker Community College Excellence Model (Figure 1) summarizes our findings regarding organizational climate, leadership, teaching, systems, and outcomes.

ORGANIZATIONAL CLIMATE

The Institutional Climate Survey, an adapted Likert scale (1967) for measuring organizational climate, was sent to a total of 731 Miami-Dade employees comprising four groups: line administrators, staff administrators, faculty, and classified or support staff. Even though the group designated as line administrators typically includes operational staff professionals, these individuals were included with the second group (staff administrators) for the purpose of this survey. Similarly, a number of employees who are typically grouped as classified

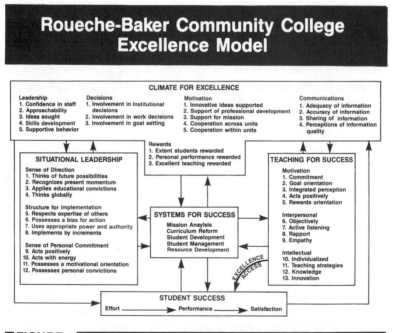

FIGURE 1

12

employees were, on the basis of their responsibilities at the college, combined with the staff administrator group. That is, only administrators whose responsibilities include clear supervision activities were represented in the line administrator sample. Therefore, the classified or support employee group represented individuals whose responsibilities were typically clerical/secretarial or nontechnical in nature. Included in the faculty group were not only full-time teachers, but also individuals on full-time faculty contracts who were not necessarily engaged in teaching—e.g., counselors and librarians. The sample was selected in the following manner: approximately one-third of each group from each of the four campuses was systematically drawn from the total employee population. As a result, 36 line administrators, 121 staff administrators, 270 faculty, and 304 classified employees received the Climate Survey. A total of 260 personnel returned the survey.

The data generated from the climate instrument indicate that there are specific attitudes, approaches, policies, and decisions which are critical to a climate of success within a community college. That is, student achievement will result from a composite, interwoven pattern, or "gestalt" of attitudes, policies, and behaviors, all consciously designed to shape a positive institutional environment. These patterns of policies and behaviors interact to create a college "feeling"; in fact, they point to specific climate factors that appear to have a significant effect on student achievement and staff productivity and satisfaction. (Further discussion of these climate factors and how they can work together to create a powerfully positive climate appears in Chapter V.)

ADMINISTRATIVE LEADERSHIP

Administrative leadership was assessed by using written self-analyses from two groups of administrators in response to open-ended questionnaires and structured interviews. The first group comprised the college executive management team, the president, the four central staff vice-presidents, the vice presidents of the four campuses, and a second group of administrators below the vice presidential level—deans, associate deans, and one director. Participation of this second group of administrators was determined by a selection process involving nominations by peers and faculty of the most outstanding administrators at Miami-Dade College. The process for selecting these administrators was handled by the college's Office of Institutional Research. Seventeen second-level administrators were selected and interviewed. All top-level administrators were interviewed. Although one campus vice president was unavailable for interviewing, a total of 25 administrators from both groups were surveyed and interviewed.

The administrative questionnaires and structured interviews were designed and developed from the literature on leadership theory. Questions were derived specifically from Brown's *Leadership Vitality* (1979). Individual responses were analyzed using McClelland's Behavioral Event Interview Technique (BEIT), a process for factoring out leadership attributes from narrative data. Results of the analyses produced a leadership competency model containing three major categories of leadership competencies: (1) sense of direction or task orientation, (2) structure for implementation, and (3) a sense of personal commitment. While the competency model is largely characteristic of exemplary leaders, it does not profess to give a full description of the characteristic leadership style of any one of the administrators interviewed. Rather, it highlights patterns of values and attitudes, as well as skills, that emerge strikingly from the group as a whole.

Therefore, the leadership model offers descriptors indicative of sound and effective leadership in general. Briefly, the model shows three major categories. The ability of an effective leader to have vision, to recognize present momentum and apply it to decisionmaking, to have educational convictions, and to think globally is indicative of the major characteristics from the first category—*sense of direction*. The ability of an effective leader to respect expertise in others, to have a "bias for action," to use power and authority appropriate to an educational institution, and to implement by increments indicates the major qualities from the second category—*structure for implementation*. Finally, the ability of an effective leader to think and act positively, to be energetic, to motivate others, and to exhibit interpersonal warmth demonstrates attributes from the third category—*sense of personal commitment*. (In Chapter VI, we discuss and provide examples of the qualities that characterize the successful leaders at Miami-Dade.)

TEACHING EXCELLENCE

Teaching effectiveness was assessed by using written teacher self-analyses in response to open-ended questionnaires followed by structured interviews of faculty members selected by peers and administrators as outstanding. In addition, all students of each selected professor were asked to rate him/her using a Likert-type questionnaire, indicating the extent to which the professor demonstrated the teaching qualities we were examining. The development of the instruments given to

Miami-Dade faculty and their students began with 12 Selection Research teaching themes (SRI, Inc., Omaha, Nebraska). Following our study of secondary education, we revised and expanded the original SRI teaching themes for assessing teaching quality at Miami-Dade. Thus, the instrument is based on our teaching excellence model, derived from the first phase of our study and consisting of the 13 themes or competencies we found that excellent instructors exhibit.

Research indicates that any one set of specific instructor behaviors does not apply to all teaching situations. A wide variety of forces at work on a given campus or in a particular classroom will ultimately determine the type of instructor behavior that is best or most appropriate. Therefore, as with the leadership model, the teaching competency model is largely characteristic of exemplary faculty and does not purport to give a full description of the characteristic teaching style of any one of the professors interviewed. Rather it highlights recurrent patterns of qualities and skills that clearly emerge in the group as a whole.

Our teaching model also has three major categories of instructional competencies: motivational, interpersonal, and intellectual themes. A professor who (1) has a strong commitment, (2) sets goals for her- or himself as well as for students, (3) sees the larger context of the subject matter, (4) has a positive regard for all students, and (5) feels rewarded when students succeed demonstrates motivational qualities. Second, a professor who (1) has an objective outlook when evaluating students, (2) is fair and listens actively, (3) establishes good rapport with students, and (4) is aware of the thoughts and feelings of others, exhibits interpersonal skills. Finally, a professor who (1) individualizes and personalizes instruction, (2) is well organized, (3) gets students involved, (4) demonstrates a depth of knowledge of his subject, and (5) is creative and innovative, possesses qualities from the third category—intellectual skills. (A complete discussion of the 13 teaching themes demonstrated by excellent professors at Miami-Dade appears in Chapter VI.)

SYSTEMS FOR STUDENT SUCCESS

Our research documents strong and powerful relationships among organizational climate, administrative leadership, and teaching excellence. These three institutional attributes become synergistic when everyone in the institution collaborates to reach for organizational and educational excellence. Collaborative efforts on a large scale have resulted in distinct curriculum reforms which account for a large proportion of the success achieved in the past decade at Miami-Dade Community College. These reform accomplishments could not have occurred without the administrative leadership and the teaching excellence found at the college.

The restructuring of the educational program at Miami-Dade began in 1978 with more modest aspirations than what was eventually obtained. President McCabe initiated a revision of the general educational program which eventually brought about a complete educational reform involving the development of automated informational systems for diagnosing, advising, placing, and monitoring students. The Miami-Dade Student Flow Model, a computerized system used to support a comprehensive program of general education, developed from the early reform efforts. (This system as well as other systems and programs developed through collaborative efforts at the college are more fully described in Chapters II, III, and IV.)

THE EXCELLENCE AXIS

Our investigative case study of Miami-Dade Community College shows strong evidence that certain leadership attributes, instructional qualities, and climate variables work together to produce programs and systems which can keep the open door open while, at the same time, achieving and maintaining quality. The use of automation combined with intense professional staff involvement and commitment has led to some solutions to the myriad learning problems posed by open access.

Our research supports the notion that administration exists in a college to establish and manage a climate which is both satisfying and rewarding to faculty and learners. Our study also confirms that teaching behaviors found to be positively correlated with high student achievement are represented extensively in the faculty at Miami-Dade. Similarly, the characteristics observed among the outstanding and key administrative leaders of the college strongly correlate with leadership effectiveness as described in the literature and by previous research. Our developmental model of community college excellence seeks to link climate, administrative leadership, instructor excellence, and support systems to measurable growth and development in learners. Thus, the excellence axis seeks to increase effort and motivation in learners and conveys the message that effort leads to performance and that performance leads to the learner's success and satisfaction.

In the following pages of this volume, specifics of the general concepts and devices outlined in this chapter are more fully described and illustrated. We believe this intensive study demonstrates that community colleges do not have to close the door in order to achieve excellence. Many models of excellence exist at Miami-Dade Community College; we have attempted to present a representative sample of them for emulation and adoption by those who wish to achieve access with quality and to offer every American the opportunity to realize his or her highest potential.

THE COLLEGE
AND THE
COMMUNITY

N inety years ago, the city of Miami did not exist; today the Miami-Fort Lauderdale Standard Consolidated Statistical Area has a population of three million people, more than the entire state of Florida in 1950. Thirty years ago, Miami-Dade Community College did not exist; by 1985 the college had enrolled 500,000 credit students and had become the nation's first community college to have graduated 100,000 students. The Miami community and Miami-Dade Community College have grown together at phenomenal rates, and the college has worked hard—and successfully—to meet the needs of the burgeoning urban area.

THE GROWTH OF MIAMI-DADE COMMUNITY COLLEGE

From Establishment to Independence

In February 1957 the Board of Public Instruction appointed a 14-member Citizens Planning Committee to lay the groundwork for a junior college. Three years later, on September 6, 1960, Dade County Junior College opened its doors to 1,428 students. At that time, Miami blacks could only attend a private college 200 miles north in Daytona Beach or the public Florida A & M University even farther away in Tallahassee. Dade County Junior College was the first integrated institution of education in Florida. At first, there was no formal campus, so the 65-member faculty held classes in various high schools and "portables." The president's office was a renovated tractor shed, and other officials were in buildings originally designed for agricultural education, specifically for housing cows. One dean and his staff were the subject of much humor because they were housed in what had been a poultry farm's laying house. Its location earned the college such nicknames as "Pig Pen U" and "Chicken Coop College."

Nevertheless, students attended the college seriously, and enrollments more than doubled the second year—to 3,556. In the spring of 1961 the college produced its first graduates, 100 with Associate in Arts degrees and 37 with Associate in Science.

In 1962 the campus moved from the chicken coops to the quonset huts of a 230-acre World War II naval air base. The 37 military buildings were renovated hurriedly over the summer, and that fall 186 faculty members met over 6,000 students. The "campus" looked like a tired military base, not a college. The cracked runways were blown with sand, and there were sandspurs instead of trees.

The next year, 1963, was a critical one for the college. Miami-Dade began its campus transformation as the construction of its first permanent building, a three-story classroom and administration building, was completed. Later that year the health center and stadium were completed. The college also got a new name: Miami-Dade Junior College. (The Junior was replaced with Community in 1973.) And once again the enrollment jumped—to 9,626—making Miami-Dade the fastest-growing college in the nation.

In 1965 Miami-Dade received its formal accreditation from the Southern Association of Schools and Colleges. It also began construction of a new campus, 23 miles southwest of the original site. Following the Miami-Dade tradition, the South Campus opened to 1,942 students in temporary quarters—high schools, a movie theater, a Sunday school building, a synagogue. Once again, faculty offices were in the ubiquitous "portables."

Nineteen sixty-five also marked a major reorganization of the administrative structure. A vice president became the chief administrative officer for each campus, in charge of the internal affairs of that campus. The president was thus freed to focus his attention on the external operations. The new organizational structure was designed for efficiency, economy, and autonomy for each campus, while the president was still legally responsible for the administration of the college as a whole.

By 1967 the student population was 23,341, the largest of any institution of higher education in Florida. These students represented more entering freshmen than the combined units of the state's university system, one of every four students in the Florida System of Community and Junior Colleges, one of every nine students enrolled in all institutions of higher learning in the state, and one of every 72 students enrolled in any junior/community college in the nation. The student body represented 44 states and 18 foreign countries.

The trend toward internationalism continued. In 1968, Miami-Dade had the fourth largest foreign enrollment in the nation; by 1969, with a total of 3,998 foreign nationals, Miami-Dade jumped to second place (with NYU still first). By 1970, Miami-Dade was in first place, with nearly 5,000 students representing 66 countries. This was a marked contrast from the first student body ten years earlier, which had no out-of-county, out-of-state, or foreign students at all.

Independence came in 1968. The Florida Legislature made all junior colleges in the state separate legal entities, no longer under the control of local public school boards. The Advisory Committee became the District Board of Trustees, and Miami-Dade Junior College was on its own.

Continued Growth and Expansion

Although there was talk of a leveling off of enrollment in the late 60's, Miami-Dade continued to grow. Enrollment was 26,863 in 1968. In 1969 it was 29,556, and Miami-Dade enrolled its 100,000th student. The faculty had grown to 918 full-time and 398 part-time members; including noninstructional staff, Miami-Dade employed a total of 2,058.

As the student body and staff grew, the campus expanded also. In 1970, a third campus opened in downtown Miami. As usual, the first classes were held in temporary quarters, but new buildings were begun within a year on what would be called the Mitchell Wolfson New World Center Campus. The new campus enrolled 1,081 students, and the total college enrollment for 1970 was 34,548.

Two new kinds of expansion came in 1971. Privately owned Mount Sinai Hospital entered an agreement with Miami-Dade and built a new Allied Health Building which was leased to Miami-Dade for $1 a year. This center accommodated the college's rapidly expanding paramedical program and brought to seven the number of off-campus extensions operated by the three campuses.

TV College made its debut that year, also. Two credit courses in ecology were presented on open circuit television. Later, other courses were added and the name was changed from "TV College" to "Open College." Meanwhile, Miami-Dade continued to build new facilities at the North Campus and the Downtown Campus.

In 1975–76 Miami-Dade's enrollment reached a new high of 40,099 credit students. Not only was Miami-Dade bigger than ever, but other changes were also becoming apparent. The average age of the students was moving up; a third of the credit students were over 25. There were more part-time students, more women, more students taking advantage of "time savers" like credit by examination so they could accelerate their progress through college. Open College, the radio-TV extension, expanded to more courses and, naturally, more students. As a result of a self-study program that ended that year, recommendations were made for major reforms in the education programs of Miami-Dade.

By 1976–77, women outnumbered men for the first time, and Miami-Dade had become bilingual and tri-ethnic. The student population was 53.3% non-Hispanic white; 27.1% Hispanic, and 18.7% black. The Downtown Campus got a new name that year—New World Center Campus. Two dedications were held, one of a classroom building on the North Campus, the other the new Medical Center Campus. In the spring, 6,100 students graduated from the four combined campuses.

More graduates, 6,492, and more buildings, two more, both on the South Campus, marked the year 1978. And during this year, Miami-Dade began to implement some of its major reforms.

Changes for the Eighties

In 1981–82 Miami-Dade finished putting into place the major reforms that had been inaugurated in 1978. The college received national awards for an Open College television series and for adaptation of the course for handicapped persons. New off-campus extension centers opened, some replacing centers that had closed, others adding new programs in new locations, so that the total was nearly a dozen. At graduation, 7,335 students (over 1000 more than in 1981) received their degrees, including the 80,000th graduate.

In the fall of 1982, the Florida College Level Academic Skills Test (CLAST) was administered for the first time. In Florida students must pass all four sub-tests in order to receive an Associate degree, or they may pass three and gain provisional entry with junior-level status at a state university. Miami-Dade developed sample tests to help students identify weaknesses in preparation for these tests. That year Miami-Dade also opened the Centers for Excellence, located at various campuses and designed to provide quality occupational preparation. These centers were directly tied to the employment needs of the Miami-Dade area.

In 1983–84, the New World Center Campus, located downtown, was renamed the Mitchell Wolfson New World Center Campus, honoring Miami-Dade's first board chairman. Upon his death, a major endowment of over $40 million was established and placed in a separate foundation, the Mitchell Wolfson, Sr., Foundation. The funds established a "margin of excellence" for Miami-Dade, the first income of which was received in 1985. In 1983–84, the college also instituted a new admissions policy, opened new Centers for Excellence, built new facilities for firefighter training and sports, and inaugurated the first "Apple Orchard" computer center for student use.

Nineteen eighty-five marked Miami-Dade's 25th anniversary. The college finished a new independent telephone system, linking the four campuses by microwave transmission. The Ford Foundation granted Miami-Dade $225,000 to follow a group of students through the college's entire program and assess its strengths and weaknesses. Miami-Dade also announced a $5 million endowment fund drive. The college had grown from 1,388 students scattered among the buildings of "Chicken Coop U" to a 1985 enrollment of 41,427 students on four modern campuses.

THE MIAMI COMMUNITY

In 90 years Miami has grown from an alligator swamp to a cosmopolitan city; Dade County has a population of approximately 1,175,000. It is a service-oriented community; in 1983 manufacturing accounted for only 9% of its total income. It is an international city, with an economy based on international banking, finance, trade, and tourism. It is a multi-ethnic city, the only one of the country's 26 largest cities that does not have an ethnic majority; the three largest groups are non-Hispanic white (48%), Hispanic (36%), and non-Hispanic black (17%). And it is a bilingual city, speaking English, Spanish, and in some cases a hybrid called "Spanglish."

Growth of an International City

When Dade County Junior College opened its doors in 1960, Miami had no foreign banks, only a few U.S. banks engaged in international trade, no trans-Atlantic air traffic, and no seaport. Today there are over 130 banks engaged in international finance. More than 250 multinational corporations have offices in the Miami area, and 65 are headquartered there. The airport is now the second busiest in the United States, handling over 20 million passengers and $4 billion in foreign trade every year. The seaport, built in 1964, handles $9 billion in foreign trade and is the world's largest cruise-ship port. T.D. Allman, in a 1983 *Esquire* article, pointed out that Greater Miami's GNP is larger than that of any Latin American country except Brazil and Mexico.

Less than 10 years ago, tourism was still Miami's biggest industry. Today banking, finance, and trade account for two-thirds of the economy, and tourism itself has gone international. In 1981 tourists from Latin America spent more than those from New York, Miami's traditional source of tourist trade. Miami has truly become an international city.

People Problems—and Solutions

With international banking, trade, and commerce have come international people and some resulting problems. Refugees and immigrants from Cuba and Haiti came in huge waves in the '80s. Racial conflicts have erupted. Crime, especially the "international" type, has risen sharply. The elderly, who once flocked to Miami as a retirement haven, are being outnumbered by the "baby boomers" and by the children of the new young arrivals.

In the years since Castro took over the Cuban government, thousands of Cubans have immigrated to the United States, and many of them have stayed in Miami. For years, officials referred to the "Cuban problem" as the refugees slowly became assimilated. But now many of them are naturalized citizens, and "in less than twenty years the average income of a refugee family of four has risen by 1,000 percent—from $2,229 in 1963 to $22,356 in 1980" (Allman, 1983, p. 46). The boat people seemed like a mammoth problem, but 90,000 of Miami's 120,000 Marielitos are gainfully employed. While most of the immigrants speak Spanish as a native language, many of them, especially the younger ones, speak English as well. The influx of Haitian boat people has been slowed, and they also are becoming assimilated.

The immigrants, both legal and illegal, moved into economic slots that had previously been filled by blacks. For example, Allman points out that in 1960, blacks owned or operated 28% of Miami gas stations, but by 1979, after Cubans had moved into that niche, the total of black-owned stations was only 8%. Meanwhile, as in many cities, urban renewal was destroying black neighborhoods and replacing them with nothing. A combination of many factors, some of them economic, led to riots in 1980. But blacks have since replaced despair with political power; black voters decided the outcome of a recent mayoral election. And blacks have often joined with other minorities (remember, in Miami everyone is a minority) to fight common problems such as crime.

Many elderly have always headed toward southern Florida at retirement time. In 1980, 16% of the population was 65 or older, significantly higher than the national average of 11.3%. The surge of working-age immigrants, however, decreased the percentages of elderly, and since 1980 the numbers of elderly have declined while the birth rate hit record highs between 1979 and 1984. Nevertheless, the recent problems with Social Security and Medicaid have been exacerbated in Miami with its large number of elderly people.

Miami has, in the last thirty years, become a city of growth, a city of diversity, and for many people, a city of immense opportunity. Miami-Dade Community College has been a part of the growth, has felt the effects of the diversity, and has provided many people the skills to take advantage of the opportunity.

IMPACT OF THE COMMUNITY ON THE COLLEGE

The nature of the community which a college serves obviously has an impact on the nature of the college. The international flavor of Greater Miami means that Miami-Dade Community College also has an international flavor; indeed, it has the largest enrollment of foreign students of any college or university in the nation. For many people in Miami, English is not a native language, and over half of the Miami-Dade students are not native English speakers. Dade County has a mixed ethnicity, and Miami-Dade's population is also a mix of Hispanic, non-Hispanic white, non-Hispanic black, and others. The economic base of the community is centered not on manufacturing or industry, but on processing of goods, money, information, and people. Thus Miami-Dade's occupational programs are aimed toward skills needed in these areas.

Miami-Dade serves its community in five basic ways. First it offers vocational and occupational skills tied directly to the needs of the community. Second, it offers programs designed with the international needs of this specific community in mind. It also offers a wide variety of social services. The Emphasis on Excellence program seeks to serve the community not only by keeping its best students in the Miami area, but also by bringing in cultural attractions that benefit the entire community. Finally, the college offers a variety of programs for junior high and high school students in the area.

Miami-Dade Community College offers a wide variety of occupational programs on its four campuses. It trains Miami's personnel in criminal justice and firefighting. It offers programs in such varied fields as ophthalmic health care, banking and finance, funeral services, air conditioning, and dental hygiene. The Center for Business and Industry on the Wolfson Campus provides a full range of training programs for businesses in the South Florida area. Since the college works closely with local business organizations, these programs are geared to the specific needs of the private sector of the community. Miami-Dade's personnel closely monitor the occupational needs of the community, listen to people and what they want, and then plan programs

27

to fill those needs, so that both the job-seeking student and the local employer are satisfied with Miami-Dade's services.

The college also tries to meet the needs of the international community. Since Miami attracts a large number of refugees, the college has always offered programs to serve them. In the early days of the college, Miami-Dade provided specialized programs in language training and employability skills for Cuban refugees. After large increases in the numbers of Cuban and Haitian refugees in 1980, Miami-Dade worked with several community agencies to obtain its largest grant ever, $3.2 million, which has provided over 8,000 refugees at various locations with the English training and employability skills they need to begin the assimilation process into the mainstream of American society.

Miami-Dade has assisted foreign or refugee students with certain specialized programs as well. The Medical Center Campus offers a specialized program to assist foreign nurses to become proficient in English and review nursing theory and practice so that they can sit for the state board nursing exams. The Wolfson campus has the Cuban Accountants Program, designed as an entry vehicle for certified Cuban accountants. The Division of Bilingual Studies on the Wolfson Campus not only helps native Spanish speakers learn English but also helps native English speakers learn Spanish, especially the Spanish they are likely to need in the workplace. In a program for these specialized Spanish needs, classes often take place at the workplace. Another program helps bilingual students learn special skills for interpretation and translation. And, of course, for all non-native speakers of English who need it, the English as a Second Language (ESL) program is available on every campus.

Miami-Dade also provides a number of social services to the community. Some of these are designed to help Miami-Dade students as well, such as the child care workers in the preschool and early childhood programs, and the dental students who offer dental work and prophylactic treatment. Other programs offer help to the mentally retarded, the physically handicapped, senior citizens, nontraditional students, and those who want help with psychological problems. There are several programs for women on different campuses. A community theater program called Prometeo not only trains students for professional careers in the performing arts but also helps the community preserve its Hispanic heritage. The Owner Building Center offers courses in affordable, energy-efficient housing to those who wish to build or remodel their own homes. A model energy-efficient structure on the South

Campus is a tangible demonstration of a valuable, non-destructive use of the environment. Of course, the college offers a number of non-credit courses, including one for ground training in ultra-light aircraft!

The Emphasis on Excellence program is designed primarily to encourage superior students to attend Miami-Dade. The program, described in detail in Chapter III, is a means of serving the community by keeping its bright young people, who will one day be community leaders, in the local area. The program also attracts outstanding professors, guest speakers, and cultural attractions. These benefits are not limited to participants in the program; the community is invited and even encouraged to attend such programs as the Lunchtime Lively Arts Series.

Finally, the college works closely with local junior and senior high schools. A Saturday Enrichment program for high school students offers the opportunity to earn college credits. The Talent Search program reaches out to students whose parents never attended college and provides them with special opportunities for the higher education and possibly better future their parents were unable to attain. The Performing and Visual Arts Center and the Miami Youth Symphony provide special advanced training in the creative arts and music for talented high school students. The Governor's Program for the Gifted and Talented provides similar support for the academically gifted.

MIAMI-DADE COMMUNITY COLLEGE TODAY

Miami-Dade Community College today is a huge system, serving some 41,000 credit students each semester. Over 51% of its student body is Hispanic, 31% is white non-Hispanic, and 16% is black non-Hispanic. Miami-Dade has more lower-division black students than any other college or university in Florida and more Hispanic students than all other Florida higher education institutions combined. Sixty percent of its students enter with deficiencies in at least one of the basic skills areas. Over 50% are not native speakers of English. There are more full-time nonimmigrant alien visa students at Miami-Dade than at any other college or university in the nation. Each year nearly 30,000 disadvantaged students receive financial aid through the college.

Miami-Dade today is a successful college in a changing community. It accepts students at all economic and academic skills levels. At the same time, it enables students to become well-rounded, academically proficient, truly "educated" people and thus to reach the goals of society, the college, and the students themselves. Miami-Dade had to change to meet these two goals. It continues to monitor both the community and itself and to adjust its programs and policies to match the needs of both the community and its own students.

C H A P T E R III

SYSTEMS FOR
SUCCESS

Educational institutions, from kindergartens to universities, experienced a multitude of problems in the 1960s and 1970s. The most critical for most schools was the problem of decreasing academic skills. Different schools had different ways of handling these problems. Some raised their admissions standards; some waited until the state legislature took over; some ignored the problem and are still where they were in the '70s; and some took matters into their own hands, found viable solutions to their problems, and instituted major reforms throughout the institution. Miami-Dade has been innovative and thorough, and the reforms the college instituted from 1978 to 1982 have worked so well that we can accurately call them "Systems for Success."

THE PROBLEMS OF THE 1960S AND 1970S

During the late '60s, our nation experienced important social changes. As the civil rights movement gathered momentum, minority students saw education as one means of gaining equality, and many colleges were eager to accept these new students. When Miami-Dade opened its doors in 1960, it was the only college within 250 miles of Miami that would accept black students (McCabe, 1984b).

Many students fought for the rights of the individual. They were influenced not only by the civil rights movement but also by the Vietnam War and those who protested the draft. This struggle for individual rights carried over into colleges—and even into elementary and secondary schools. Students wanted the right to determine course content, the right to select their own courses, the right to take their own chances. They rarely consulted faculty advisors or degree plans; self-advisement was the rule, and often all courses the student chose to take, even the remedial courses, were counted toward graduation. The number of courses, rather than balanced selection or quality, became the criterion for a diploma or other academic credential. As a result, few students were meeting any standards other than those they imposed on themselves. Academic standards were decreasing rapidly and steadily. Dr. Robert McCabe, President of Miami-Dade, says,

33

Perhaps this situation grew in reaction to the concern of many minorities that the educational systems did not provide a ladder to success, but rather created discriminatory screening mechanisms which were used to prevent them from acquiring the credentials necessary to participate fully in society (1984b, p. 1).

Admission standards, prerequisite courses, and minimum competencies were some of the policies seen as barriers. When these were eliminated, students were able to progress quickly through the educational system to receive their credentials and enter the world of work. Many were thus able to compete for professional positions for the first time, and in the late 1960s, when the civil rights movement was in full swing, minorities with academic credentials were eagerly recruited by businesses, schools, and other institutions.

How did these changes in the social setting change education, especially education at the college level? First, they affected the admissions process. Many colleges changed their admission requirements so that their doors were more open and they could admit a wider variety of students, including minority students who might not have been able to meet the high academic standards formerly required. Community colleges especially were strong supporters of this "open-door" policy, and most community colleges today retain a commitment to an admissions policy that allows virtually any student who so desires to enter the college.

As a result of this open-door policy, many students entered college with academic deficiencies. After a lifetime of gathering credits rather than learning basic skills, they were unprepared for the more stringent demands of college courses. Yet many of them perceived their unexpected failure at the college level to be the fault of the college, not of themselves or their educational background.

The open-door policy also meant that colleges became more diverse. Large numbers of minority students began to attend college. Foreign students, poor students, and older-than-usual students, some who already had considerable career experience and others who had not been in school in 20 years, all applied to and were accepted at the community colleges. And they all ended up in the same classes, along with the traditional young, nonminority, academically skilled student.

Once they were admitted, many students found themselves in considerable academic trouble. Since they were deficient in one or more basic skills, they had trouble meeting the rigorous demands of college courses. Thus they failed—in large numbers. They were frustrated by their failure, by their own lack of skills, and by their inability to reach the goals of a diploma quickly and easily.

Many faculty members found themselves in trouble also. The great diversity of students called for a greater degree of individualization, but the range of skills had become so wide that many professors found it virtually impossible to provide materials at enough levels. And many professors didn't feel that it was their responsibility to teach a sophisticated college course in, say, chemical engineering or philosophy to a student who had trouble with basic math or reading. The teachers felt they had two choices: to teach at the college level and have a large number of withdrawals and failing grades, or to lower their standards and teach at a level that many of them found professionally unacceptable. Either way, the professors were frustrated.

The academically deficient students were not the only ones hurt by these policies; the academically gifted were also penalized. If the standards were lowered, the able students were not challenged and did not receive the education they were capable of and had paid to receive. If standards were kept high, then more advanced classes often didn't draw enough students to warrant keeping them in the schedule. When the classes were dropped, the few students who had registered for them were penalized.

The problems of varying skills in a class were exacerbated by the so-called "right to fail" and by the open-access system of self-advisement. Students who felt that admissions standards and skills testing were barriers to a well-deserved education also felt that they had a right to try anything they chose. Unfortunately, this right often ended up being the "right to fail." Rather than following a prescribed sequence of courses, they selected classes in whatever order they chose. Thus, a student was "self-advised," rather than advised by a faculty member or a required sequence, and he had "open access" to the entire curriculum, since there were no prerequisites. A student who planned to be an engineer might register for calculus, never having had (or having passed) advanced algebra. Without the prerequisite skills, he was likely to fail the course. As they wished, students did indeed have rights and freedoms—the right to attempt whatever they wished at their own risk, the freedom to select their own courses, unrestricted by college or departmental rules, and freedom from remedial courses, cut-off scores on achievement tests, or even advice.

In spite of the drawbacks of all these rights and freedoms, many people today still feel that the colleges' responses to the demands of the 1960s and 1970s were appropriate for the time. The civil rights movement made people conscious of the rights of minorities and the need for many Americans, previously excluded from the mainstream, to "catch up." A college diploma was often a key to open doors that allowed people to catch up, and colleges were aware of that. But the solutions of the '60s and '70s don't fit the problems of the '80s. The critical problem today is not how to open professional, civic, and economic doors for disadvantaged Americans, but how to raise low academic standards while maintaining the traditional commitment to an open door.

Financial considerations also enter the picture. Partly as a result of the civil rights movement, the federal government began providing financial assistance to great numbers of students. Today over half of Miami-Dade's students receive some form of financial aid, for a total of over $14,000,000. After the Vietnam War, some returning veterans felt entitled to everything the government offered, including educational grants. However, they did not feel obligated to attend classes or demonstrate academic achievement. Other students were influenced by their example and began to accept the financial aid without any of the obligations it was meant to entail.

In the 1960s and early 1970s, when college enrollments were rapidly increasing, their enrollment-driven budgets were fat, and colleges could afford to expand programs, campuses, and faculties. However, as enrollments have leveled off or declined in the '80s, budgets have done likewise. But the items for which those budgets paid have often not decreased. Overhead per student, expensive faculty salaries, and building costs have remained the same—or gotten higher. Lower-salaried teaching employees often must be dropped, class sizes increased, and potential new programs postponed or cancelled. The money crunch often means that colleges need to sustain enrollment in order to maintain financial stability.

Faced with these problems, some colleges decided to raise their costs and/or their admission standards, in effect partially closing their doors. When only academically able students can get in, the college can maintain high expectations and standards. When costs are high, students (and parents) want their money's worth. They often want a directive policy, not an open-access curriculum. Most colleges had additional motives for higher admission standards and costs. One was size; they simply didn't want to admit many more students because they didn't want to get much bigger. They liked the 500 or 5,000 students they had. And costs were going up, even if the student body didn't increase.

But community colleges, especially today, are faced with a fundamental dilemma. On one hand, they want to keep their doors open to everyone; on the other hand, they want to offer quality and academic excellence in their programs. The open-door, open-access, right-to-fail mentality of the '60s adds to the dilemma of the '80s.

HISTORY OF THE REFORMS

If the old open-door model doesn't work, what does? Miami-Dade spent three years in a self-study trying to answer that question. In 1978, the college began instituting reforms that would establish a new model, accommodating both the open door and high academic standards. The program is now much more directive. It includes assessment after admission, a required general education core, standards of academic progress that students must meet in order to remain in good standing in the college, increased feedback to all students, and support for those who need assistance to be successful. The program relies heavily on computerized technology at all levels. By 1982, the new programs were in place, and by 1985, Miami-Dade had data that indicated the programs were a success.

In 1975, Miami-Dade began to study possible reforms, partly as a result of the self-study required in 1974 for accreditation by the Southern Association of Schools and Colleges. It was clear that fundamental change was necessary in order that the school keep its dual, but somewhat paradoxical, goals of open door and high academic standards. Committees were created, representing the faculties of all four campuses. These committees held town meetings, read articles, discussed goals, drafted documents, analyzed issues and responses, and finally made a series of proposals. The college also applied for and received a federal grant of $900,000 through Title III of the Higher Education Act of 1965. Much of this money was used to design and implement a computer system that provides individualized support and feedback in various parts of the reform structures.

Implementation of the reforms was gradual so that the college had time to train teachers, develop course materials, redesign support services, and revise the new courses after trial runs. The first innovation was the Standards of Academic Progress, which were instituted in 1978 for all new students. These standards required that students maintain certain minimal grade averages and pass half of all courses for which they registered. If they did not, a system of warning, probation, and suspension would be enforced. A student's progress was continually monitored once he or she had completed seven hours. In 1979, these standards were phased in for all returning students.

Basic skills assessment was also implemented in 1979. After students were admitted, they were given tests to assess their basic skills. Those students found deficient were advised to take developmental courses to increase those skills. Certain minimal skills were required for entry into some core courses, and students who were deficient in basic skills were encouraged to take a light course load and concentrate on those skill deficiencies. Support services were available in the form of special courses (such as study skills and time management), writing labs, and individualized computer programs designed to help students improve specific skills.

In the fall of 1981, the general education courses were implemented. All new degree-seeking students were required to take five "core" courses in general education. These classes were designed not as introductions to majors or specific disciplines, but as interdisciplinary courses that would help students learn about themselves, the world around them, and their relationship to that world. These courses would provide the basic general education that the Miami-Dade committee found was fundamental to a true education and that had been missing in the self-advised, "open-access" system.

Miami-Dade Community College found that the reforms worked. The results will be detailed in Chapter IV, but in general the students liked the innovations, and both achievement and enrollment are rising. In 1984 the college completed another detailed self-study, resulting in a new set of recommendations for change and improvement. One change already in place is a writing requirement in every course. Detailed requirements are specified for some courses, but every professor is asked to require some writing as a basic objective of the class. Thus students see that communication skills are necessary for every phase of education and career interest, not just for English courses.

DIRECTIONS OF THE COLLEGE

The reforms at Miami-Dade had several purposes. The college wanted to effect certain fundamental changes which would benefit the students and, indirectly, the faculty. Rather than tying itself to specific objectives, the college formulated a series of general directions or purposes:

1. To raise expectations for student effort and performance. The college expects students to come to class regularly and to work hard enough to meet at least the minimum requirements of each course. Simply registering for courses (and, in many cases collecting financial aid) isn't enough. Since Miami-Dade is a publicly funded college, and since many

students receive financial assistance, every student is dependent on the taxpayer for the benefits of college. Therefore, reasoned the college, every student is obligated to repay this debt to society by performing to the best of his or her ability. The public has invested in the college because the training which the college gives should benefit the public. Most students feel this obligation; they understand that college is a job, not a gift. They approve of higher expectations, and as a result, they show higher achievement.

2. To provide more direction and fewer choices. Students no longer have "open access" to the curriculum. Instead, the college specifies levels of achievement necessary to take classes, requires developmental work for those who need help achieving this level, and sets out the courses which a student must take and the order in which they must be taken. Students are given considerable assistance in selecting not only the courses appropriate for their skills but also an appropriate number of courses, so that a working student will have enough time to devote to studies. As a result, both students and faculty are likely to experience success rather than failure.

3. To provide more information and feedback to students. Since the college has increased expectations and become more directive, it must provide individualized information about a student's progress. Students need to know whether they are meeting the expectations, and they need information so that they can follow the directive course plan established by the college.

4. To provide increased instructional and personal support to those who are having difficulties. Those who are deficient in academic skills cannot expect to complete a program with high expectations (such as an Associate degree) in the same time as those who have no academic difficulties. The college not only helps with developmental programs so that students can work directly on those skills areas with which they are having difficulty, but also provides a system in which course loads are reduced, so that students can spend an appropriate amount of time and effort studying for the courses they do take. Finally, extensive effort is made to train faculty to individualize instruction, since the range of skills within a class is now limited to a workable range.

5. To maintain a focus on academic achievement. The college holds a strong commitment to achievement and academic excellence, so that a degree from Miami-Dade symbolizes a high and recognizable level of performance. Academically gifted students are also provided with expanded opportunities so that they will stay in the area, develop their skills, and contribute their talents to the community.

6. To set a clear point at which a student must show academic progress or leave the college. Students at Miami-Dade are given ample opportunity to get support, both personal and instructional, and improve their academic standing. They receive considerable feedback about their progress—or lack of it. If all of the college's systems do not result in a minimum of academic progress, then the college must conclude that it can no longer do that student any good. It is clear that the student is not going to succeed in college at this time, and the college is no longer justified in allowing further public investment. Consequently, the student is suspended from the college. The point must be clearly set, ample warnings must be given, and then the policy must be enforced.

THE REFORMS

Miami-Dade made reforms in eight basic areas:
1. Curriculum reforms, including general education courses,
2. Assessment testing,
3. Basic skills support,
4. Emphasis on Excellence, an honors program,
5. Standards of Academic Progress,
6. Academic Alert, a feedback system about academic standing,
7. Advisement and Graduation Information System, and
8. Faculty and staff development.

Curriculum Reforms

General Education

In a sense, Miami-Dade made only two changes, but these were so significant that everything else had to be changed to support them. One was the decision to require general education courses for every degree-seeking student. The second was to set minimum standards for academic performance.

"General education" has been loosely defined over the years to mean either "all courses not directed toward a student's career interest" or "those common courses required of everybody." Robert McCabe, now the president of Miami-Dade, and Jeffrey Lukenbill, Dean of Academic Affairs, wrote a booklet in 1978 called *General Education in a Changing Society*, in which they define general education, present a rationale for its use in a community college, and state 26 goals of general education, grouped into six categories. From this framework, the General

Education Department developed a three-tier program of core courses, distribution courses, and electives, all of which met general education goals and were specifically not directed toward major fields of study or particular career goals.

Lukenbill and McCabe define general education at Miami-Dade Community College as

> that aspect of the College's instructional program which has as its fundamental purpose the development and integration of every student's knowledge, skills, attitudes, and experiences so that the student can engage effectively in a lifelong process of inquiry and decision making (1978, p. 29).

Why general education? Supporters of general education have attempted to provide a rationale based on assumptions about students needing a broad background, exposure to different subjects, and/or a "well-rounded" education. They maintain that students need this general knowledge base in order to proceed to more specialized disciplines. But even supporters often neglect to specify the values they think will be derived from a general education. Detractors of general education maintain that education is not meant to deal with students' "personal" lives, but is, instead, preparation for a career. According to these critics, college has a purely economic function. Students come to college in order to get good jobs; anything not directly relevant to the student's major may be elected as a course outside that major, but should not be required.

Lukenbill and McCabe argue that these statements are superficial, at most indicating positions that support implied values. According to them,

> a rationale for general education at Miami-Dade Community College should be based on the mission and goals of the College, the nature and needs of the community, the needs of its students, and the significant changes likely to take place in society in the near future. Fundamental to this rationale are value statements (p. 30).

The authors present five statements of values that answer the question, "What is the worth of general education?"

"*A general education should enable individuals to integrate their knowledge so that they may draw upon the many sources of learning in making decisions and taking action in daily practical situations*" (Lukenbill & McCabe, p. 31). In order to cope with the complexities of modern society and to enhance the quality of their lives, individuals need to be able to integrate cognitive knowledge, psychomotor skills, and affective attitudes. As a result of this integration, they will be better able to make informed decisions, including the political and social decisions of citizens and voters.

"*A general education should provide students with a beginning or a further commitment to a lifetime of learning*" (p. 31). Since our society is constantly changing, since knowledge is increasing at phenomenal rates, since storage and retrieval of information have become a part of our everyday technology, and since the future, related to career opportunities, is uncertain, individuals need to be able to learn. A general education is not a termination, but an initial phase in a lifetime of necessary learning.

"*A general education should enable students to intensify the process of self-actualization*" (p. 31). Individuals need to understand that they can and should direct their own lives. Particularly in a complex, urban society, everyday stress can cause job dissatisfaction, mental and physical illness, and discontent with life in general. The individual who learns to cope with the sources of stress and find fulfillment in spite of stressful forces will lead a happier, more productive life.

"*A general education should enable students to find value in the activities and experiences of their lives, both those in which they engage because of obligations or commitments and those which are discretionary in nature*" (p. 32). While evidence indicates that family life is becoming less stable, individuals need to find value and satisfaction in family relationships. Similarly, research indicates that there is increasing job dissatisfaction among those in the "highest" jobs as well as those who are underemployed or who have repetitious or uninteresting work. A general education should help both employers and employees understand the means by which workers can find satisfaction in their jobs. Finally, Americans can look forward to increasing discretionary time, but they need to be prepared to use this time in ways that are satisfying and valuable. Creative endeavors and aesthetic experiences can be more important to Americans, who no longer have to struggle for basic survival needs, but can look further up the hierarchy of needs for satisfaction.

"*Finally, general education should increase students' understanding of the breadth and depth of ideas, the growth of society and institutions, and the development and application of the scientific process in communities throughout the world*" (p. 33). As Lukenbill and McCabe explain,

> Mankind has progressed by expanding ideas, and individuals
> must be aware of this progress if they wish to realize their own

intellectual potential. Likewise, students need a historical perspective to be able to evaluate the significance of events and to make judgments concerning current events as they develop. In an age which is so widely influenced by science and technology, individuals must also understand the scientific process if science is to remain a means for progress and not the master of our lives (p. 33).

America is fortunate to have an abundance of material goods, but we have also gotten used to this abundance and tend to squander our national resources. At the same time, other countries are able, through communications technology, to see the difference between their standards of living and ours, and they are reaching for their fair share. Students should understand not only the natural environment and its resources, but also the need for conservation and equitable distribution of those resources.

Lukenbill and McCabe's twenty-six goals of general education, grouped into six categories, are necessarily broad and cannot all be met by one class. However, they provide guidelines, especially for core courses, so that specific objectives and skills that meet at least some of the general education goals can be determined for each course.

The first four goals deal with fundamental skills: (1) "The students will be able to speak, listen, write, and read competently and in an organized and critical manner;" (2) "The students will be able to communicate effectively with individuals in different aspects of their lives." The authors make the point that these two goals are the responsibility not only of English or communications teachers, but of all teachers. These goals should be addressed in some manner by every course. The other two goals, dealing with computations and logical decision-making processes, are also fundamental and should be addressed in all classes where they are appropriate.

The second set of goals focuses on the individual. It deals with self-direction, the nature of man, physical and mental health, use of discretionary time, prejudices, and aesthetic and creative activities.

The next four goals deal with the individual's aims for the future. These goals are concerned with the students' abilities to analyze and assess their personal values and life goals, to investigate career choices, and to set educational objectives in view of their tentative or definite career choices as well as other noncareer pursuits.

Four goals refer to the individual's relationships with other persons and groups. These are concerned with the individual's knowledge of interpersonal skills and the application of those skills, especially in relation to family, organizations, and other cultures and ethnic groups.

The fifth set of goals is concerned with society and the individual. These goals deal with the students' knowledge of the contributions and philosophies of various societies and individuals to contemporary society. Two of these goals refer specifically to United States society, the ideas which have affected it, and the social principles which govern it.

The last set of goals deals with natural phenomena and the individual. These are concerned with the individual's knowledge of scientific methods and principles, his interaction with the natural environment, and the effects of technology.

With the rationale and goals of education clearly stated, the General Education Committee at Miami-Dade recommended three "tiers" of courses for all candidates for an Associate of Arts degree. First, a group of five core courses would be required for all degree-seeking students, including those who were not planning to transfer or continue their education past the community college level. In addition, those seeking an A.A. degree would be required to select five additional second-tier "distribution courses" from limited lists of general education options. Only two courses would be electives or third-tier courses, chosen from a broad list of electives having general education objectives. These twelve courses would make up the 36 general education credits required for an A.A. degree; another two credits would be required in physical education/health maintenance. A total of 62 hours are required for a degree; 38 of them would be in general education, directed by the college.

General Education Curriculum

All students are required to take the following five courses:
1. Communications
2. Humanities
3. The Social Environment
4. The Natural Environment
5. Individual Growth and Development

The Communications course focuses on writing skills not only in expository essays, but also in correspondence, outlines, reports, and other kinds of writing. Logic and organization are also stressed. This course emphasizes more advanced skills than the minimum competency required for entrance to the course.

The Humanities course is multi-disciplinary, focusing on achievements in art, literature, music, drama, architecture, and philosophy. Students are encouraged to participate and develop a lifelong interest in aesthetic, creative, humanistic ideas and forms of expression.

The Social Environment course emphasizes the social, economic, and political institutions which have helped shape U.S. society. Students study philosophies, lifestyles, and historical developments which have had an influence on their own ways of life, and they develop an understanding of the various cultures.

The Natural Environment course focuses on the history and development of scientific ideas. The philosophy of science, including scientific methods, is discussed in relation to various natural sciences. Emphasis is on the importance of technology and specific scientific issues in students' own lives and environments.

Individual Growth and Development is a course focused on individual psychological and physical well-being. Students learn to assess factors and plan when making decisions, including decisions about their own careers. They study psychological and sociological concepts such as prejudice, personal values, family relationships, and group dynamics. The course also emphasizes such aspects of physical well-being as nutrition, substance abuse, and stress reduction.

All core courses are expected to emphasize broad, universal concepts rather than specific details. They are to be cross-disciplinary and thus are taught by professors from across the college curricula. Each core course is clearly tied to one specific set of general education goals, although all core courses are expected to include the fundamental skills goals, especially the two concerned with communications.

Distribution Courses

Most students do not have a choice of the distribution course that follows Communications. In response to faculty concern about the quality of student writing, most students are required to take a course in English Composition which follows the Communications course and focuses on longer essays and other forms of writing. For those few students who demonstrate proficiency in writing at this level, other distribution courses are available—Creative Writing, Speech, and Introduction to Literature.

All distribution courses are meant to meet General Education objectives. They should emphasize broad principles, major themes, problem solving, important issues, and relationships with other disciplines. They should not be designed as specialized courses in one major area of study or for a particular career plan. Each campus has its own list of distribution courses available on that campus; the following list is a sample, not a complete list. Each student must select four courses (12 hours) from these groups, including at least one course from each group.

HUMANITIES	SOCIAL SCIENCES	NATURAL SCIENCES
Art	Anthropology	Biology
Drama	Economics	Chemistry
Foreign Language	Geography	Earth Sciences
Literature	History	Mathematics
Music	Political Science	Physics
Philosophy	Psychology	Interdisciplinary
Interdisciplinary	Interdisciplinary	Natural Sciences
Humanities	Social Sciences	

The two elective courses may be chosen from a wide range of options. The only requirement is that the class meet several of the general education goals. Different campuses have different course selections. Since most courses in arts and sciences meet this requirement, students have an opportunity to explore individual interests while meeting general education requirements.

Physical Education Requirement

The Health and Physical Education Department decided to take advantage of the nation's interest in fitness and combine it with Miami-Dade's reform movement. In the past, students could choose any two of a wide variety of activity courses, ranging from tennis to scuba diving to aerobics. However, these courses did not give students a chance to explore why exercise and fitness are important, nor did they offer an opportunity to develop an individual lifetime activity plan. Also, the faculty needed more information about students before helping them plan individualized exercise programs.

With these factors in mind, a new course called Health Analysis and Improvement was implemented in 1979. The student may now choose two activity courses or the new health class. With the implementation of this course, the college removed all exemptions, including those for age, handicaps, or other conditions. Since Health Analysis has proved helpful to those students who have taken it, advisors recommend the course to all students.

In the initial phase of the health course, data is gathered about the student's medical history and physical condition. The student not only fills out a questionnaire, but also takes a series of tests that analyze blood pressure, lung capacity, grip strength, and body composition (percentage of body fat to height and weight). A computer-generated individualized letter is sent to each student, and he or she is assisted in developing an individualized training program. The remainder of the course is a series of classroom and laboratory sessions. In the classroom, students discuss such topics as nutrition, stress, and the body systems. In the laboratory, they can participate in various exercise and activity programs.

Finally, the student's health is reevaluated, and another individualized letter is sent with a comparison of the two sets of laboratory results. This letter also includes suggestions about maintaining the exercise program initiated during the course.

Assessment Testing

Students enter Miami-Dade with a broad variety of skills. In fact, this wide range of skills had been one of biggest problems of the pre-reform days. Miami-Dade officials had also identified serious skills deficiencies as a critical problem facing the college. Thus, assessment testing was to determine the level of an individual's basic skills.

After students have been admitted to Miami-Dade, their skills are assessed by the Comparative Guidance and Placement (CGP) Test. This placement test determines the level of a student's skills in reading, mathematical computation and written English expression. The results are used, together with information from other sources such as high school transcripts, to give the student a picture of his or her own strengths and weaknesses. The college assumes the responsibility of matching the student to the appropriate educational program. Some students need developmental work to improve skills; some need to go directly into the core courses; others need the challenge of an advanced program.

The assessment testing program was implemented gradually, beginning in spring 1979 and becoming fully implemented by fall 1981. Today it is required of all first-time-in-college students carrying nine hours, students who have earned fifteen or more credits, and students wishing to enroll in any math or English course. Thus, in effect, it is required of all students.

Students who are not native speakers of English may take a different test. However, they must show sufficient proficiency in English before they can take college-level courses; otherwise they must take intensive training in English until they can demonstrate that they are proficient enough to be successful in a course that is taught in English.

Basic Skills

If the results of the CGP show that students are weak in one or more areas, they must take developmental courses to improve their skills in that area. They are restricted in other coursework and in their course load. Students must successfully complete the developmental work before moving on to the core curriculum in Communications (required for an Associate degree). Students who already demonstrate sufficient proficiency may enroll in the core course in Communications immediately.

What is a minimum proficiency level? A variety of factors go into making this decision:

> As a very broad indication of the proficiency levels that will be a minimal requirement, students may be expected to read and comprehend material in a metropolitan newspaper and to write a short paragraph containing sentences without serious errors in grammar and punctuation (Lukenbill & McCabe, 1978, p. 48).

More specifically, students scoring below the 30th percentile on the Written English Expression portion of the CGP and 55th percentile on computation are required to complete developmental course work before enrolling in college-level courses such as the Communications core course and introductory algebra. Lower scores are accepted in reading, although all those with a score below the 32nd percentile are strongly encouraged to take reading.

Students who took the SAT or ACT can present those scores in lieu of CGP scores. A combined score of 840 on the SAT or 17 on the ACT exempts the student from developmental course work.

Miami-Dade is trying to focus not on the skills a student brings into the college, but on the skills he has when he leaves. Many students demonstrate deficiencies when they enter, and their skills level must be brought up. How long that takes depends on the students and their initial skills; the college provides a wealth of individualized and computerized support services, which will help students improve their skills so that their degree represents successful completion of truly college-level courses, not an accumulation of credits in watered-down courses. Since this skills work is required, and since students who need developmental work are also required to cut down on the number of courses they take, many students need three to five years in order to complete a "two-year" degree plan. Getting through in a hurry is not on Miami-Dade's list of priorities; getting through with a high level of achievement is.

Emphasis on Excellence

Students who demonstrate a high level of achievement on the CGP tests are invited to enter an honors program called "Emphasis on Excellence," designed to attract and serve superior students. These students often become community leaders in various fields, and the program is one way to encourage them to remain in their own communities for higher education.

The Emphasis on Excellence program tries to meet the special needs of these students in a number of ways from financial assistance to special classes to unique programs. The program includes eight basic components:

1. Scholarships to superior students who are entering college for the first time. These "High School Achievement Awards" are granted to Dade County high-school graduates who rank in the top 10 percent of their graduating class. The awards are worth approximately $1,000 to students who earn an Associate Degree at Miami-Dade. Of course, students must meet certain academic requirements, but if they do so, they not only continue to receive scholarship money, but are also given special assistance to secure more financial help when they complete their Associate degrees and transfer.

2. Scholarships to students who are already at Miami-Dade and demonstrate high achievement during their freshman year. One hundred students from the four campuses are selected for these awards each year.

3. Honors classes and opportunities for accelerated programs. Miami-Dade provides special honors classes which focus on independent learning, active participation, and higher achievement than that expected of students in the regular curriculum. Students benefit from the challenges that appeal to both their aspirations and their potential; faculty benefit from the challenges and rewards that result from working with gifted students; the college as a whole benefits from the guest speakers and faculty and from the attitude of high expectations and outstanding achievement associated with the program.

Outstanding students also have opportunities to accelerate their college programs. They may choose to enroll concurrently in both high school and some college courses. They may choose to take tests allowing them to receive college credit for high scores, or they may take intensive immersion courses. All of these programs offer students the possibility of completing their Miami-Dade studies in less than the traditional two years.

4. A series of lectures and credited seminars by nationally known speakers and artists. Such guests as Edward Albee, Maya Angelou, Alfred Eisenstaedt, Michael Tilson Thomas, and Edward Teller have spoken to large groups, small workshops, and individual classes.

5. An entertainment series called the Creative Focus Program, which presents various forms of performing arts, thus enriching not only the students and faculty of the college but also the community. Some performances are by the students and faculty of Miami-Dade; others are by nationally known artists and productions. The Creative Focus Program also sponsors the Lunchtime Lively Arts Series, in which performers and artists attract students, downtown employees, shoppers, and tourists to share lunch in a cultural atmosphere. Creative Focus also works with local high schools to supplement their fine arts programs.

6. The Summer Program for the Gifted and Talented. Two hundred 10th and 11th graders are selected each summer for an intensive six-week program in selected areas such as physics, creative writing, or computer science. The program is designed as a "hands-on" experience.

7. Unique programs at each Miami-Dade campus. Each campus offers special courses and/or programs that parallel its own areas of specialization. Medical Center Campus has offered seminars in such areas as medical ethics and aging; South Campus has offered week-long programs on the role of the computer in modern America; Mitchell Wolfson New World Campus has published a literary magazine, held literary contests, and presented special programs on the law, featuring local legal figures; North Campus has offered a varied selection of specialized honors courses and other special activities.

8. Intensive language and cultural experiences in foreign countries. Students usually complete various reading and writing assignments before and after their trips, which take place during the summer term, and receive 3–9 semester credits in such courses as foreign language, music, humanities, or social science. The total immersion in the country's language and culture adds considerable depth to the learning experience.

Standards of Academic Progress

Some of the general directions in Miami-Dade's reform study involved higher expectations, higher achievement, and setting a minimum level at which students were expected to achieve. Of course, these directions imply not only specific minimum standards, but also some means of requiring that they be met. The result is the Standards of Academic Progress, a system of warnings, probation, and finally suspension for low grade point average or excessive withdrawals from classes.

Although the standards may sound like a penalty system, they actually work more as a support system. Beginning in the semester in which seven credits are earned, a student's progress is continually monitored. If the student withdraws from more than half his or her classes, or his or her GPA falls below 1.5, the student is notified of a change in academic status (warning, probation, suspension, etc., depending on the number of hours for which the student has registered). More important, the student is notified at the same time of ways to improve that status. Some ways are not optional. For example, the student's course load is limited for the next semester, so that more time can be spent studying well for a few courses. (While this restriction may increase the time required for the student to complete a degree plan, it also increases the chances of eventual successful completion.) Other suggestions are made, such as developmental courses, special laboratories, counseling, or programs that help with study and time management skills. The purpose is to help students succeed in college by telling them when they are not doing well and then giving them both time and help to improve. As Lukenbill and McCabe put it, "There is abundant history of students who begin poorly but who eventually are successful. These cases may represent the college's more important achievement" (1978, p. 26).

However, while the college has a responsibility to help students succeed, the students themselves have a responsibility to take advantage of the assistance offered them. If students wish to take advantage of the educational opportunities offered by a tax-supported college, they must show a commitment by staying in class and keeping their grades up. Otherwise, they are wasting the public's money and everyone's time: "Students who cannot or do not make satisfactory use of the College's educational services cannot be permitted to drain the College's and the public's limited resources" (Lukenbill & McCabe, 1978, p. 95).

Miami-Dade recognizes that circumstances may change; therefore the standards allow for readmission after suspension for one major term, provided the student makes a 2.0 term average and earns credit in at least half the classes for which he or she is registered. Even after the academic dismissal, the student may petition for readmission if he or she can present evidence that circumstances have changed and readmission is warranted.

Academic Alert

Academic Alert and Advisement is a computerized system that gives all students feedback about their progress. Computer-produced individualized letters are sent out about six weeks into the term. These letters inform students that their academic progress and attendance are "satisfactory" or "not satisfactory" in specific courses. The computer program gathers information about the student's credit load, previous performance, native language, basic skills, and then, through another sophisticated computer program, generates a personalized letter to each of Miami-Dade's thousands of students. This letter also includes information about the student's current academic status and counseling on courses for the following term.

The Academic Alert system is useful in three basic ways. First, and most important, it monitors student progress through a term. The letter serves as a kind of intervention because it informs students about a potential problem early enough for them to do something. And the letter also tells them *what* to do about it. This "early warning" system, coupled with suggestions for improvement, helps students get out of academic trouble before the end of the term.

Second, the Academic Alert system provides information that an advisor can use to help a student select appropriate courses. Finally, it informs campus personnel about the numbers of students likely to fall into certain categories (such as "satisfactory in all courses" or "needs improvement in some courses") and provides information about the number of students who will be referred to basic skills labs or other support services. Thus personnel can begin early to make decisions concerning scheduling, numbers of sections, numbers and kinds of personnel needed, and so forth.

SAMPLE LETTER 1

Miami-Dade Community College
South Campus
300 N.E. 2nd Avenue
Miami, Florida 33132

March 3, 1981

Student's Name
Address

Dear Student:

It's good to have you back at Miami-Dade South. I hope that the information provided in this letter will help you successfully complete your courses and register for an appropriate schedule for next term. Although we do not send a progress report during spring or summer terms, you should know that you will receive an academic alert letter during both fall and winter terms.

(Student's name), your grade-point average of 2.79 indicates successful work. I am encouraged by your demonstration of academic achievement.

Your instructors report that your academic progress and attendance so far have been satisfactory. Congratulations—I hope that you are building on this good start.

Registration for the next term will begin on March 30th. It is time to plan your class schedule for next term. Although you indicated this term that you are not a degree-seeking student, you may want to discuss your course selection with an advisor. Come to career planning and advisement, Room 3113, telephone 596-1125, for assistance if you want to consider the possibility of switching to a degree or certificate program. Or, if you wish help by departmental advisors, pick up an advisement location list in Room 3113, or telephone 596-1125. Since you have already earned 30 or more credits, you are encouraged to review degree requirements with the career planning and advisement staff, Room 3113, telephone 596-1125, before your next registration.

Keep this letter to bring with you when you discuss your academic progress with your instructors. I hope you find this information helpful and I wish you success at South Campus.

Sincerely,   Student ID

Barbara M. Kranz
Director, Career Planning and Advisement

SAMPLE LETTER 2

Miami-Dade Community College
South Campus
300 N.E. 2nd Avenue
Miami, Florida 33132

March 3, 1981

Student's Name
Address

Dear Student:

Welcome to Miami-Dade South. Since this is your first semester at South Campus, I hope that you are now involved in our college and are ready for an academic progress report. The following report will alert you to how you are progressing this term and help you make decisions about your program of study.

So far at least one of your instructors has reported that your academic work needs to improve (see list below). You should discuss your course progress with your instructor. Your problem may be also caused by your enrollment in too many courses. You may want to consider getting additional help, limiting your outside activities, or planning additional study time. It has been noted that your attendance needs improvement. You should try to go to all classes as scheduled. Please discuss your attendance with your instructors.

Improvement is needed in your performance and attendance in: SSI1011.

Keep this letter to bring with you when you discuss your academic progress with your instructors. I hope you find this information helpful and I wish you success at South Campus.

Sincerely,   Student ID

Barbara M. Kranz
Director, Career Planning and Advisement

SAMPLE LETTER 3

Miami-Dade Community College
South Campus
300 N.E. 2nd Avenue
Miami, Florida 33132

March 3, 1981

Student's Name
Address

Dear Student:

I am pleased to see that you enrolled at Miami-Dade South Campus this semester. However, because you registered for 18 credits, but earned only 0 at the end of your last semester of attendance, you have been placed on academic probation. This means that you will be limited in the number of credits you can register for and that you need to select your courses carefully to avoid any further withdrawals.

Currently, you are enrolled in 4 course(s) for 12 credit(s). At least one of your instructors has reported that your academic work is satisfactory but your attendance needs improvement. At the same time, at least one of your instructors has not reported any information on your performance. We strongly urge you to discuss your progress with your instructor(s).

Progress is satisfactory in: AVM2512, PUR1000
No information is available about your progress in: AVM1022, BUL2111
Attendance is satisfactory in: AVM2512, BUL2111, PUR1000
Attendance needs improvement in: AVM1022

The number of credits you are currently carrying exceeds the credit limitation imposed by the college. Although I encourage you to complete all of your courses satisfactorily this term, you may be hurting yourself by taking too many courses. It is our experience that students who follow credit limitations can improve their academic standards.

Since you are on academic probation, you will need to see a counselor in room 1640 before you can register again. You need to be very careful in your

(Continued on page 56)

course selection and be sure you discuss your academic difficulties with your counselor. You will be limited to 9 credits in fall and winter and 3 credits in spring and summer until you improve your academic standing. We have many services to help you, and together we can come up with ways to improve your academic performance.

In closing, (student's name), let me say that you and I share the basic goal of making your college experience as rewarding as possible. This letter, with its analysis and recommendations, reflects my continuing interest in supporting you in the achievement of your goals. Please bring this letter with you the next time you meet with your faculty advisor or your academic support services counselor. Best wishes for success in the future.

Sincerely,   Student ID

Castell Bryant
Division of Academic Support Services

Advisement and Graduation Information System (AGIS)

As part of the feedback and information to students that is one of Miami-Dade's goals, the Advisement and Graduation Information System (AGIS) is the heart of the academic advisement program. AGIS provides detailed information about the individual student, such as assessment test scores and status under the Standards of Academic Progress. More important, it is a transcript showing which courses the student has registered for and the student's final status in those classes (a passing grade, withdrawal, failure, incomplete, etc.). A third important function of AGIS is to show students which courses they need to complete their programs at Miami-Dade. In fact, the transcript is rearranged to show the classes they have taken matched with the courses they need, rather than showing the courses taken in the usual chronological order. Students are thereby informed about their progress toward a particular program and what classes they need to complete it.

AGIS also lists the courses required for smooth transfer to the upper-division universities within the state, so that students can be sure they are meeting the transfer requirements as well as those for graduation from Miami-Dade. This is particularly important because of the Statewide Articulation Agreement between the university and the community college systems. This agreement specifies that the general education requirement of the baccalaureate degree is the sole responsibility of the institution granting the Associate of Arts degree. Once the A.A. is awarded, the university cannot require any more general education requirements. However, the university is responsible for courses in the major field of study. Therefore, the community college, working in conjunction with the state universities, must provide students with an accurate list of required and suggested courses, by major.

Advising students has become a relatively simple matter for faculty at Miami-Dade. The combination of the Academic Alert letter and the AGIS printout tells the advisor not only what the student's academic status currently is, but also what courses, restrictions, and/or support services are needed and why.

Student Flow

With these changes, Miami-Dade no longer has an open-access type of student flow. Instead, student flow is highly directed (see model in Figure 2). Through the use of assessment testing each student is guided into an appropriate level of course work. The Academic Alert system helps students remain successful at their level. The AGIS system monitors and provides feedback about students' progress toward their goal. Although students still have options about programs and some electives, at no point are they left to flounder through a mass of course offerings, some of which will do them little good in reaching their objectives.

Computerization

It is evident that Miami-Dade Community College has taken full advantage of computer technology; it is an information-processing college in an information-processing community.

Virtually all the college's reform programs are tied to sophisticated computer programs. RSVP (Response System with Variable Prescriptions) is the computer-based instructional management system that allows for so much individualization. It is also used to support innovative methods of serving the deaf and blind. Individual faculty members can use the system to generate materials for core or distribution courses.

RSVP is also responsible for the individualization of the Academic Alert letters. A total of 150 messages are written for the four campuses. Out of this pool, RSVP selects appropriate messages according to programmed decisions: "The possible combinations of the messages for students' letters add up to 26,878. In other words, the system can generate 26,878 unique letters if students' information is equally unique" (Anandam, 1981, p. 1).

The Health Analysis and Information course uses RSVP to individualize the letters that report the results of the fitness tests and suggest an exercise program for each student. Again at the end of the

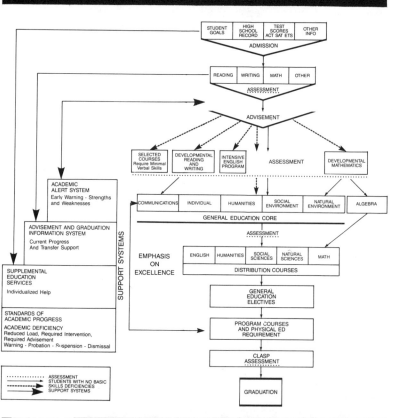

Associate in Arts Student Flow Model

FIGURE 2

term, when new tests are done, RSVP enables each student to receive a personalized comparison of the results of the two sets of tests.

Computer programs also keep track of all the information used to generate an AGIS report. The system generates outlines by major and university for each of the nine state universities and four large private colleges in Florida. Thus students can compare requirements for different colleges as well as see their own progress in meeting those requirements. There are 72 different Associate in Arts programs that will transfer to one of these upper-division institutions. AGIS can produce a document that matches an individual student's coursework with a specific degree program at Miami-Dade and the transfer requirements for that individual's desired college or university. And, with the "magic" of computer technology, AGIS can produce an up-to-the-minute printout at a terminal in the academic advisement offices of any campus. All the computer needs is a student number.

Faculty Development

To succeed in its reforms, Miami-Dade needed the support and cooperation of the faculty. Curriculum changes, the Academic Alert letters, the emphasis on basic skills, the increasing use of computers, the emphasis on high expectations and achievement, the use of AGIS for advising students—some of these required special training and some merely changes in attitude. But all required changes on the part of the faculty.

The initial description of the general education program included a section on implementation (Lukenbill & McCabe, 1978, pp. 103–04). In this section, the authors noted that faculty support was critical to the success of the reforms. They proposed that faculty members currently teaching in the content areas of the core courses be the principal developers of the course objectives and content. However, faculty from a wide variety of other content areas, including vocational and technical areas, should also participate in developing the core courses. Faculty would suggest or develop materials and teaching strategies, and workshops and seminars would be held to help teachers become familiar with the new courses. The courses would be taught on a trial basis at first, so that they could be evaluated and refined after they had been piloted. Part-time faculty would also receive substantial assistance in implementing the new curriculum.

These plans were carried out almost to the letter. First, an ethnically balanced steering committee of both men and women was formed; half its members were administrators who were experts in staff development and the other half faculty representing all the major content areas. This committee worked for approximately a year on various aspects of the reforms, but as the reforms were bound to cause conflict, they were presented as an institutional decision, not a faculty decision. And, indeed, reactions to the reforms were varied: some people were skeptical, others adopted a wait-and-see attitude, and still others firmly supported the whole idea.

Once the idea of the reforms was introduced, faculty input was used in setting course objectives, course content, and evaluation procedures. Five committees of about eight people each (all faculty, no administrators) were formed, one for each core course. Each committee had an appointed chairperson, and half the committee members were appointed, half elected. These committees had complete autonomy in developing the courses. At the same time, the administration made a commitment to staff development. If the curriculum changes required that faculty work in new areas or develop new materials, then time and training would be provided. Faculty members were given release time from teaching duties so that they could meet in seminars to develop materials. The next semester, other faculty members were released to receive training so that they could use the new materials effectively. Considerable attention was paid to methods of individualizing instruction. Faculty audited each other's classes or team-taught to become familiar with other disciplines and teaching methods. Teachers and trainers also tried to prepare for problems with students who had basic skills deficiencies, for a wide range of abilities within each class, and for needs of students of varying ethnicity.

As a result of the staff development, resource books were developed for each core course. More important, the administration was successful in convincing the faculty that the success of the core courses depended on the teachers. Faculty developed the objectives, the resource books, and the training seminars. Eventually the faculty became so committed that they recommended the seminars be required for everyone who taught the courses. The administration felt that *requiring* the seminars was not feasible, but they were pleased with the enthusiastic support of the faculty. Once the new courses were in place, the faculty decided that the courses deserved more prestige; consequently, now anyone who wishes to teach them, even part-time faculty, must "qualify" to teach core courses. Since required courses are not usually very popular with college faculties, Miami-Dade accomplished an unusual feat that has been good for the college and the students.

Faculty support was necessary for smooth implementation of other reforms as well. For example, the Academic Alert system will not work well without faculty cooperation, since the system is based on information from teachers about the performance and attendance of students half-way through the term. However, the faculty apparently sees the importance of the Academic Alert feedback and supports the idea, since 95 to 98 percent of some 3,000 instructional staff turn in the necessary information on time. Faculty also learned to use computers well enough to get AGIS reports to use in the advising process, and now nearly every faculty member is involved in advising, and every student is required to be advised.

Obviously, without faculty support, the curriculum changes, the Academic Alert system, the basic skills requirements, and all the rest would not have much chance of success. With strong, enthusiastic faculty support the reforms have been implemented gradually by informed teachers who were determined to make them work. And they have.

Continuing Reform

Since its initial set of reforms, the college has been continually on the alert for possible improvements. Some things have been simply fine-tuned. Others have been changed in major ways, especially as the Florida legislature mandated changes that affected all the state's community colleges. And in 1984, Miami-Dade undertook another major self-study, again as part of the accreditation process of the Southern Association of Schools and Colleges. This self-study resulted in eight volumes, including one for each of the four campuses, and examined every part of the college program. Included in these volumes are new goals, recommendations, rationales, and projected timelines, proof that reform is not a one-time event, but a constantly changing process and that reforms are not set in concrete: the reforms themselves can be changed as well.

Thus, some adjustments have been made on the core courses. The Natural Environment was renamed "Energy in the Natural Environment," and Individual Growth and Development was renamed "The Individual in Transition." Content of all the core courses was changed slightly in response to student feedback. The Communications course was recently renamed "English Composition I," and the second level course, "English Composition II." The list of distribution courses was adjusted for different campuses. Although relatively minor, these changes demonstrate Miami-Dade's commitment to continuing improvement.

The Florida Legislature mandated some requirements that caused Miami-Dade to make more substantial changes. In 1982 the College Level Academic Skills Test was administered for the first time. Commonly known as CLAST, this test is required of every student planning to begin a junior year in a state-supported university. The sophomore-level test consists of four subtests, in reading, objective writing, essay, and mathematics. The objective writing section contains multiple choice questions about writing; the essay section asks students to actually write a short composition. By the 1984–85 year, students had to pass three out of four sections in order to continue in the state university system, and they had to pass all four in order to receive an A.A. degree. In 1986 and again in 1989 minimum scores will go up, so that students must demonstrate even higher skills than they do now in order to get their A.A. degrees and/or go on to a state university. Both community college transfer and "native" university students must take this test before continuing, and community college students who are graduating are required to take it as an exit competency test.

The legislature also decided that assessment tests should be mandatory for every incoming student. They drew up a list of tests from which each college or university could choose the particular test(s) it wanted to use.

The legislature also mandated specific course requirements. The "Gordon Rule," named for Florida Senator Jack Gordon, requires that students write a minimum of 24,000 words in college courses before entering the junior year. In addition, a mathematics course that includes elementary algebra is now required of all students.

Miami-Dade responded to the mandates in a variety of ways. Before CLAST was given for the first time in the fall of 1982, Miami-Dade had already developed a pre-CLAST assessment so that students could see the areas in which they were weakest. They could then take developmental courses or get special help in the skills laboratories before taking the real CLAST. Miami-Dade also used the results of the CLAST tests to uncover the weaknesses in their own program. The biggest weakness turned out to be in writing. Researchers were busy trying to determine the causes of the weakness when the legislature instituted the Gordon Rule for minimum writing requirements.

The combination of unsatisfactory test results, a legislative mandate, and Miami-Dade's own search for academic excellence led to a new emphasis on information skills. Based on the idea that "Academic (information) skills have become the most important occupational skills" (McCabe, 1983a, p. 1), new requirements call for every student seeking an Associate in Arts degree to take English Composition III as part of the general education requirements. This course replaces one of the general education electives and will come near the end of the student's program. It will emphasize writing, obviously; in fact, it requires a minimum of 6,000 written words. The other two core courses in English, Composition I and II, also require a minimum of 6,000 words each. The four core courses in other subject areas require students to write a minimum of 1,500 words each in order to receive a grade of C in the course. Finally, as part of the emphasis on "Information Skills for an Information Age," *all* courses are now required to include reading and writing objectives as part of the stated course goals.

Composing requires a higher level of thinking than responding to objective questions. Students usually must work harder and think more to produce good writing than to answer "multiple-guess" questions. Thus, the college anticipates an increase in application, analysis, synthesis, and evaluation skills as a result of the new writing requirements. It is still too early to judge any long-term results, but a short-term effect was a 50% reduction in the number of test forms processed in 1983–84, the first year of the new writing policy. Obviously, teachers are requiring more writing in lieu of objective tests.

In conjunction with the new requirements, Miami-Dade is providing extra support for both students and faculty. New writing labs for students who are having difficulty are available on every campus. Since many faculty members have lost some of their own skills in assigning and evaluating written composition, courses and workshops for faculty are being offered on each campus. These staff development services help faculty see how writing assignments can be incorporated into each course, provide faculty with support materials, and provide training in assigning and evaluating written work. Support materials have been expanded so that there is now a complete resource book on "writing across the curriculum." And, with the help of the Florida Legislature, class size has been reduced; now grading compositions has become feasible (as it is not when there are 50 to 150 students in a single class).

The legislature also required a math course for all college graduates. This course was incorporated into the general education requirements for which community colleges are responsible under the Articulation Agreement. When the math course and English Composition III were included in the general education requirements, students lost the two electives which originally constituted the third tier of the general education program. Instead, all candidates for an A.A. degree must now take eight required courses (the three English composition courses, one math course, and the four core courses), four distribution courses (chosen from the specified lists), and two credit hours of health or physical education. These requirements equal 38 hours of the 62 required for an A.A. degree; thus students still have 24 hours for electives or courses in their major field of study. And those 38 general education hours ensure that every student have the solid background in general skills and information that Miami-Dade has determined is one of the goals of a college education.

When the legislature determined that in 1985 all colleges should administer an assessment from a list of state-approved tests, Miami-Dade's CGP test was not on the list; therefore, the college chose the Florida Multiple Assessment Program and Services (MAPS) instead and established interim placement scores until the statewide scores became effective in July 1985.

In the 1984 self-study, Miami-Dade did a thorough analysis of its programs and policies. Some recommendations concern what Miami-Dade should keep, the core courses and the Academic Alert system being two programs that are considered highly successful. Some recommendations address what should change, but none of them is as sweeping as the reforms that arose from the self-study of the mid-'70s. The most serious college-wide problem identified in the 1984 study seems to be communication among the members of the college system about the programs the college already provides. The recommendations address ways to improve communication and increase the knowledge of the students, faculty, and general public. Other recommended changes are "fine-tuning" and deal, for example, with what courses should be on the distribution course list, not whether there should be distribution courses. Some of the recommendations are for studies to be made to determine if further action should be taken. Some of them call for more unity among the four campuses. Some are long-range goals, looking into 1990 and beyond. But the most impressive point is that the 1984 self-study offers virtually uniform support for the major reforms that were made. General education and other curriculum changes, assessment testing, developmental courses, the Standards of Academic Progress, the Academic Alert System, and the AGIS System all received strong endorsements from students, faculty, administrators, and the community.

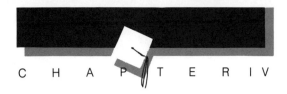

OUTCOMES

D
id Miami-Dade's reforms work? In a word, yes. According to its 1984 self-study committees, Miami-Dade's general education program, educational prescriptions, and student support systems

> were found to be meeting the objectives for which they were designed, confirming the principal assumptions of the reforms that increased direction, control, and support of student performance comprise effective strategies for addressing the open access/academic quality challenge faced by Miami-Dade (Preston, 1984, p. 234).

Whenever an institution makes changes, it needs feedback to see if the changes have been successful, if they have accomplished their purpose. Unfortunately, some institutions neglect to gather data to find out. They believe that Change X is going to bring about Result Y; thus they institute Change X and then assume Change Y has occurred. Miami-Dade doesn't make that assumption. Instead, their Office of Institutional Research gathers data from a wide variety of sources to find out if Change Y did indeed occur, and often to find out *why* it did or did not. The various committees of the Institutional Self-Study in 1984 also gathered considerable data, especially attitudinal data, about the reforms.

RESULTS OF SPECIFIC REFORMS

General Education

One of the most controversial of Miami-Dade's original reforms was the decision to implement general education for all students.

> At issue was the commitment by Miami-Dade Community College to an integrated general education curriculum rather than early professional and disciplinary specialization. Also at issue was the basic belief that these five core courses helped students make syntheses, see patterns and systems, understand general theories and ideas, and integrate life with learning, while providing a foundation for later specialization in professional or disciplinary training and for life (Roberts, 1984, p. 57).

67

The resulting tiers of core courses, distribution courses, and electives are still in place, and the directions and goals of general education are still fundamental guidelines for Miami-Dade's educational philosophy. They serve as the foundation of the whole competency-based model of general education, in which the objectives, teaching strategies, and materials for each course are tied to the general education goals which that course tries to meet.

For the 1984 self-study, respondents in a number of surveys were asked to label ten concepts as "very important," "important," or "not important" to be taught at a community college for success after graduation. These concepts were paraphrased or inferred from the goals of general education. The result was that all ten items were endorsed, most by overwhelming majorities. The strongest endorsement went to the first goal, the fundamental skills goal that reads, "To help students improve their ability to write, speak, think, and listen." A range of respondents from 79% (CLAST examinees) to 100% (local agencies) considered this goal to be "very important." Even the lowest-ranked item on the list, "To help students improve the ways they use leisure time," got at least a 50% endorsement from every group. It is evident that the goals of general education are still relevant and important.

A look at the objectives and content of the core courses indicates that the rationale for general education is also understood. Most of the faculty (76%) believed that the objectives related to the goals, and 90% of the core course instructors stated that they based coursework primarily on the college-wide course objectives and covered all or most of the objectives in their individual classes.

Students also indicated that the core courses helped them achieve the goals. The core courses had varying degrees of influence in different goal areas, from a low of 20% for A.A. students concerning participating in organizations other than social clubs, to a high of 91% of A.A. students regarding increased ability to write.

> Particularly high percentages were given by all surveyed students to increased communications skills—89% to increased writing ability, 81% to increased speaking ability, 86% to increased thinking ability, and 82% for increased listening ability (Roberts, 1984, p. 53).

Only four items influenced fewer than 50% of all the students surveyed, and those items included registering to vote, working for political objectives, making better TV selections, and participating in nonsocial groups. In the area of basic skills, basic knowledge, and personal growth, a majority of students reported considerable influence by the core courses. Both faculty (83%) and students (78% to 82%) thought the core courses had a "positive impact" on Miami-Dade students (Roberts, 1984, p. 68).

Most students also reported that they found the core courses enjoyable, and most faculty believed that core courses should be required of degree-seeking students. Most students and faculty agreed that the core courses should remain the same, but 49% of the students wanted more latitude in distribution and elective course selection. Four percent of the students wanted radical change in the entire general education program (Roberts, 1984, p. 60). Most students found the core courses intellectually demanding and thought most of the material was new or necessary.

The core courses have been in effect only three years (they were put into place fully in winter 1982). However, at this time most people are well satisfied with them and do not think they should be changed in any major way. In fact, both students and faculty have given a resounding endorsement to the idea of required core courses and to the specific content and techniques of the Miami-Dade courses.

The distribution courses are also well accepted. Neither faculty nor students wanted the lists of distribution courses changed significantly. They agreed that the lists provided enough choices for students, although there was some concern that the new requirements for math and English classes might interfere with students' elective choices. Two of the biggest issues concerned the perceived purpose of the humanities courses and the need for a procedure for qualified students to "place out" of at least part of the required composition sequence.

New requirements related to distribution courses are, of course, hard to measure. At this time, some of the new writing requirements have been in effect less than a year. Whether these requirements will help improve CLAST scores, which is their purpose, is also difficult to determine at this time.

Placement Testing

Although Miami-Dade has recently switched to a state-selected placement test called Multiple Assessment Programs and Services (MAPS), the college has previously used the Comparative Guidance and Placement Tests (CGP) to assess students' abilities in basic skills. The results of these tests have led to student placement in developmental courses, the regular core courses, or the honors program. Since Miami-Dade is an open-door institution, many students have scores that are low enough to keep them out of the state university system as freshmen. In fact, when over 6,000 first-time-in-college students were given the CGP in the 1983 fall term, 48% scored below the placement score in reading, 42% in written English expression, and 44% in computation.

Our two main questions regarding outcomes involve, first, whether assessment testing is effective and accurate, and second, whether faculty and students believe such testing is important and worthwhile.

Volume II of the 1984 self-study summarizes the empirical data about Miami-Dade's use of the CGP (Garcia & Romanik, 1984). In one study, correlations between CGP reading and writing scores and student grades in three core courses were low to moderate. However, these correlations are in line with those reported by other institutions in the CGP norming sample and by other research that has tried to predict grades by using achievement tests. Though relatively low, the correlations do show a positive relationship between test scores and grades in core courses.

Another kind of measure determines the minimum assessment test score required to make a C in a given course. The mean predicted minimum test scores were 20.3 for reading and 23.3 for writing, which were very close to the actual placement scores of 19 and 22. Thus the placement scores had a definite correlation with the minimum requirement for a course grade.

A third kind of measure involves the proportion of correct placements (i.e., the "hit rate") using test scores. In the fall terms from 1981 to 1984, the CGP averaged a 75% hit rate in the required English composition course (ENC 1101), with a high of 79% in 1982. The average hit rate for the reading test was not available, as there is no single course for which reading scores are targeted. However, other data have shown that as reading scores increase, so does the percentage of students achieving a grade of A, B, or C in the general education courses.

A number of students should have been placed in developmental courses because of low reading scores (1–10) but were placed in core courses instead. This finding surprised some study committee members, since these low scorers should have been locked out by the computer from registering for core courses (Roberts, 1984). Of these 86 students, only 47% (or 40 students) were able to earn a grade of C or higher. Seventy-one percent of the core course enrollees scored in the highest range of reading scores and 25% in the middle range. Of those in the highest reading range, 64% to 73% made grades of A, B, or C. Predictably, those in the middle reading range made lower grades; 48% to 65% made grades of A, B, or C. Of those in the lowest reading range,

51% made a grade of C or higher in Humanities, but only 33% made a C or better in the Energy in the Natural Environment course. These numbers tell us that reading scores are correlated with grades—the higher the score, the higher the likely grade. Courses with more demanding reading requirements will obviously be harder for poor readers than courses which are heavily experiential, such as the Individual in Transition core course. Indeed, the highest grades made by poor readers in core courses were in the Individual course. That some students who score quite low can be successful in core courses may tell us several things. One possibility, of course, is that grades are inflated. Another is that the system is flexible enough to allow even some very low-scoring students a chance to succeed, if the faculty advisor believes that the scores should be overridden.

How do people feel about the validity of the CGP? The faculty accepted the basic assumption that placement in class is related to test scores. In fact, 73% of the faculty supported the use of placement testing and the resulting greater control over student academic choices (Garcia & Romanik, 1984). However, 76% of the faculty (88% of the communications faculty) felt that a writing sample should be included in the assessment process, especially since CLAST includes a writing sample. Although most faculty indicated that 20% to 50% of their students had inadequate skills, the distribution of grades indicated that 67% of the grades are A, B, or C (Garcia & Romanik, 1984). A probable cause of this discrepancy is grade inflation, a problem we will discuss in more detail later in this chapter.

Students, especially those most affected (i.e., those taking developmental courses), supported the use of placement tests. However, students do not agree with the validity of the CGP. Most of them (64%) felt that scores and classroom performance were unrelated, perhaps because students didn't receive sufficient explanation of how scores are used in course selection. In spite of this disagreement in principle, 70% of the students agreed that the writing, reading, and mathematics courses they took were appropriate for their skills levels. And those who completed the communications and mathematics courses in which they were placed by entry assessment

> had a greater probability of success in composition courses, including the Communications core course, and in required mathematics courses. Therefore the study committee [the Student Flow Subcommittee of the 1984 Self-Study] concluded that students should follow assessment prescriptions in communications and mathematics (Roberts, 1984, p. 142).

Developmental Courses

Developmental courses are the heart of an open-door college. It is through these courses, in theory at least, that students whose skills are so poor that they can't get into restricted-admissions schools are able to remediate their skills deficiencies and then successfully complete college-level work.

Are developmental courses effective? That is, if students take developmental courses, do they "catch up" so that they can be successful in college-level courses? The answer is, "It depends." It depends on how many developmental courses a student needs; it depends on how we measure success; it depends on many factors other than the developmental course(s).

In general, students who are deficient in only one area are more likely to be successful than students who are deficient in two or more areas. "Students enrolling in two or three developmental courses in their first term were more likely to drop out and had a lower retention rate than students enrolling in a single developmental course" (Garcia & Romanik, 1984, p. 50). It seems quite logical, in fact, that students who are weak in several skills areas would have difficulty progressing through college. No matter how good the developmental courses, they simply cannot provide enough training in one or two semesters to make up for years of deficiencies. It seems logical too that "students who score below the 25th percentile on standardized examinations do not graduate as often as those who score in the top quartile" (Losak, 1984b, p. 1).

However, further research by Losak and Morris (1983b) indicates that "if the students did not take remedial work during the first term, their retention rate is equal to or greater than the graduation and retention rate for the students who did take remedial courses during the first term" (p. 3). This could be an indicator that developmental courses did more harm than good, or at least did little good. However, students who self-select out of developmental courses "may not only require less remediation as a group, but also differ on several characteristics important to success in college, such as motivation, previous education, future academic plans, and attitudes toward school" (Garcia & Romanik, 1984, p. 50).

Developmental courses may not be the answer for every student, but something in the college experience at Miami-Dade is. A 1984 study looked at 195 students who were initially ineligible to enter the State University System (SUS) but had a satisfactory 2.0 or better GPA over the first two years of college. These students were eligible to graduate, dependent only on CLAST performance. They wrote the CLAST in September 1984, and of the 195, 50% (97 students) passed all four subtests. Another 54 passed three subtests, so that 151 students had attained sufficient scores to transfer to the SUS. In fact, about 30% of the students who are successful on the CLAST are students who had deficiencies when they entered Miami-Dade. Since the SUS does not admit freshmen with even one skills deficiency, these students have accomplished, through an open-access college, what they could not have accomplished otherwise—entry into the SUS.

The Office of Institutional Research at Miami-Dade has done considerable research on the relationship between students who score low on the CGP (and therefore need and/or take developmental courses) and on the CLAST. "Using the criterion of passing three or four of the CLAST subtests, there is a clear difference in performance based on whether a student took developmental coursework in one, two, or three areas" (Losak, 1984b, p. 1). Students who took one developmental course were as likely as students who took none to pass three out of four. Of the students who received remediation in only one area, 86% passed three or four subtests; of those who took no developmental courses, 93% passed. But of the students who took developmental courses in two areas, only 63% passed, and of those who took courses in three areas, only 43% passed three or four subtests. However, when the criterion is raised from three out of four to four out of four subtests, the scores show a different pattern. In this case, taking even one course makes a difference, so that 73.6% of those who took no developmental work passed, but only 57.8% of those who received remediation in one area. "There is the distinct possibility that if the student took one developmental course, that area remains weak and is the one out of four failed on the CLAST" (Losak, 1984b, p. 2). For many students, that weak fourth area remains a considerable barrier, since current standards require that a student pass all four subtests in order to receive an A.A. degree, although passage of only three will allow the student to enter the SUS.

However, we can look at this data from another, more positive perspective. Of the students who took developmental courses in two areas, 63% passed three out of four subtests. Of those who took developmental courses in one area (i.e., those who had a skills deficiency in one area at entry), 57.8% passed all four subtests. These are students who would otherwise not be in college at all, since they were initially ineligible to enter the SUS. Large numbers of students are successful in remediating their deficiencies while at Miami-Dade, and thus the college succeeds in accomplishing its dual basic objectives—maintaining an open admissions door while requiring high academic quality.

Whether developmental courses actually help in the long run (and the time between the courses and CLAST is often a fairly long run of two to four years—or more), or whether student success is due to other factors in the college experience, students and instructors *think* the developmental courses help. In a self-study survey of 1,324 developmental/ESL students, a whopping 93% of the students who were taking developmental courses indicated that the course in which they were presently enrolled increased their chances of future academic success. Over 70% believed they could not complete college without developmental instruction (Garcia & Romanik, 1984). Faculty support of developmental programs was also strong. Eighty-seven percent of the staff felt the developmental courses were effective, and 97% felt the college should continue its commitment to such programs.

The Developmental Subcommittee of the 1984 self-study notes that "the examination concerning the effectiveness of developmental instruction...has developed as many questions as it has answered" (Garcia & Romanik, 1984, p. 64). The committee calls for several changes, among them more empirical research, a consensus about a definition of "successful completion" of a developmental course, and competency tests to be required for exit from the course(s). It is clear that an open-access college needs to know whether the developmental courses in which it puts so much faith really work, and right now Miami-Dade doesn't know. However, the data are somewhat "contaminated" by the data on English as a Second Language courses and non-native speakers, making it difficult to get a clear and accurate picture. The college believes, as Dr. McCabe says, "that many students remain in the system and are successful because they took the developmental courses and simply would not be there at the end if they had not taken them" (personal communication, August 14, 1985).

Standards of Academic Progress

The Standards of Academic Progress (SOAP) were enacted by Miami-Dade in 1978. In that first year, 6,153 students (14.2% of the student body) were placed under SOAP restrictions. However, at the end of the fall term 1979, only 12% were in negative SOAP categories, and the percentage came down another point by the end of fall 1980, and still another point by the end of fall 1981. By the end of 1981–82, the pattern of students within SOAP categories had shifted, so that there were more students in the warning category and fewer in the probation and suspension categories (Ossip, 1984).

Actually, SOAP has been a three-part reform. The system has been refined twice since it was originally implemented. There are now more categories, and the categories have been redefined. As a result, more students are in the "warning" category and fewer are "clear," and more are in the "probation" category and fewer are suspended. The effect of these changes focuses on giving more support and earlier alert to students experiencing academic difficulties, especially those approaching graduation without sufficiently high GPAs.

One of the purposes of a system like SOAP is to set a point beyond which the college will not go. In other words, the college is willing to warn, intervene, offer academic help, restrict course load, and advise, but if the student's performance doesn't improve after all the college's attempts to help, the college will suspend the student. The college, as a public tax-supported system, has no obligation to continue providing services to students who have not indicated the willingness or ability to take advantage of them. Because some people were already in the system before SOAP was implemented, the first fair comparison of suspension rates was between fall 1979 and fall 1980. The suspension rates of all ethnic groups declined, and the suspension rates for black students declined by an impressive 44%.

Since Miami-Dade has an enrollment-driven funding formula, the budget decreases as the student body does. In the first two and a half years of SOAP, nearly 8,000 students were suspended. When the numbers are adjusted for voluntary withdrawal, the college lost about 5% of its total enrollment due to SOAP suspension. In one sense, the college lost $1,500,000 in state and federal funding each year. In another sense, the college saved the taxpayers that much each year by not allowing nonperforming students to continue enrollment.

SOAP seems to be accomplishing its purposes. In spite of the suspension of over 15,000 students from 1978 to 1985,

> completion rates and retention have actually increased, as many students were helped to remain in the system who, in earlier years, would have quit in despair. To illustrate, one study

showed that of the full-time students who entered the College in the fall term of 1977, 46% were either graduated or enrolled three years later. For a comparable group in 1981, 53% were either graduated or still enrolled three years later (McCabe, in press).

Of those students who were suspended between 1979 and 1984, approximately half eventually returned.

Under SOAP, students who remain in college three of four terms in a two-year period (persisters) have improved GPAs or fairly similar GPAs to "pre-SOAP" students. Black students showed significant improvement in GPAs from 2.00 (pre-SOAP) to 2.25 (post-SOAP). On the other hand, more students who are nonpersisters are dropping out after one term, but these students have lower GPAs. Again, the standards are serving their purpose of raising the academic performance of those students who are willing and able to perform in college work. "As part-time students accumulate sufficient credits to come in contact with the Standards, more are deciding that college is not for them" (Losak & Morris, 1983, p. 4). Although numbers vary from one ethnic group to another and depend to some degree on how long students continue to re-enroll, the general conclusion is that "students appear to be changing their college-going behavior based on information received through the Standards. Those who continue appear to be achieving at a higher level, and less talented students are discontinuing" (Losak & Morris, 1983a, p. 8).

Many people were concerned about the impact of the reforms, especially SOAP, on retention and graduation rates of minority students. During the first year that SOAP was in effect, retention and graduation rates did indeed drop for all ethnic groups. But by 1979, three-year retention and graduation rates had returned to their former, pre-Standards level, and for black students the 1979 rates were much higher—a 25% increase in the three-year graduation rate over those entering in 1976. In Figures 3, 4, 5, and 6, the 1976 group represents the last group not affected by SOAP. The 1977 group was given a year of grace before impact. The 1978 and 1979 groups were affected immediately upon enrollment. These charts were made in 1982, after the 1979 group had been at Miami-Dade for three years (Losak, 1983, pp. 5–6; McCabe, 1983b, pp. 7–8).

How do people feel about SOAP? All of the groups surveyed by the 1984 self-study committees indicated a favorable reaction to SOAP. In fact, 81% to 87% of the students in nonclear SOAP categories, over half of the students in clear SOAP categories, and 65% to 69% of the staff, administrators, and faculty agreed that SOAP is an effective means of identifying students who experience course difficulties. The faculty have also reported that students have become much more

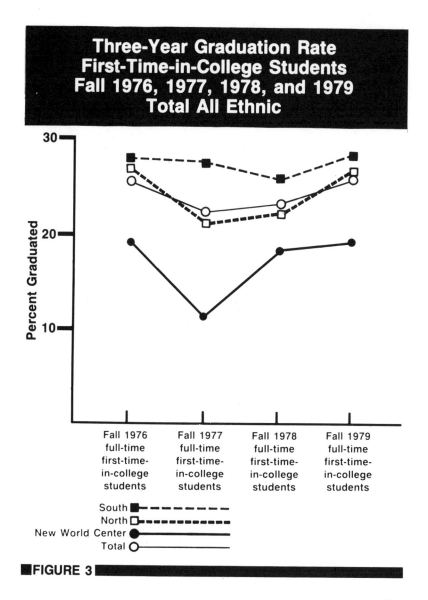

**Three-Year Graduation Rate
First-Time-in-College Students
Fall 1976, 1977, 1978, and 1979
Total All Ethnic**

South ■
North □
New World Center ●
Total ○

■FIGURE 3

serious about their studies and about their programs with the SOAP system in place. Most students and faculty thought the categories were appropriate and understood the SOAP restrictions and registration processes. Most students thought SOAP should recognize outstanding

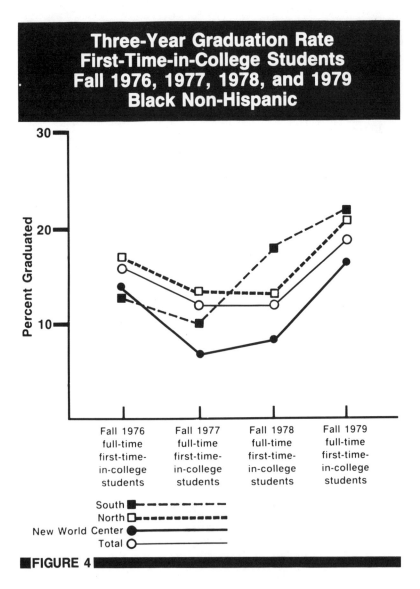

**Three-Year Graduation Rate
First-Time-in-College Students
Fall 1976, 1977, 1978, and 1979
Black Non-Hispanic**

■FIGURE 4

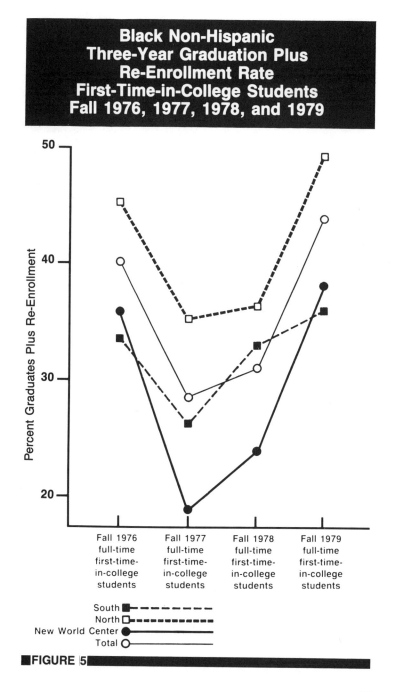

**Black Non-Hispanic
Three-Year Graduation Plus
Re-Enrollment Rate
First-Time-in-College Students
Fall 1976, 1977, 1978, and 1979**

Percent Graduates Plus Re-Enrollment

Fall 1976
full-time
first-time-
in-college
students

Fall 1977
full-time
first-time-
in-college
students

Fall 1978
full-time
first-time-
in-college
students

Fall 1979
full-time
first-time-
in-college
students

South ■ — — — — — —
North □ ● ● ● ● ● ● ● ●
New World Center ●
Total ○

■FIGURE 5■

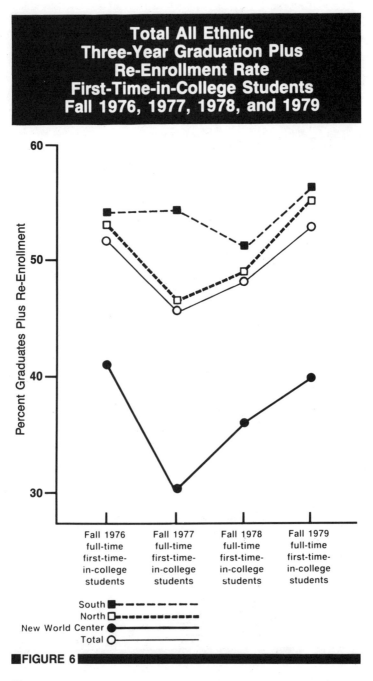

**Total All Ethnic
Three-Year Graduation Plus
Re-Enrollment Rate
First-Time-in-College Students
Fall 1976, 1977, 1978, and 1979**

FIGURE 6

student performance as well as unsatisfactory performance. Perhaps the most important survey responses involved the use of money to continue funding for SOAP: 76% of the students and 60% of the faculty approved continued funding, whereas only 18% of the students and 10% of the faculty disapproved. In fact, the self-study's recommendations about SOAP involved communication and understanding rather than major changes (Ossip, 1984).

Academic Alert

Academic Alert is the system of sending individual letters to each of Miami-Dade's 40,000 or so students in each of the long terms (fall and winter) informing students of their status in each course, based on both grades and attendance. The letters, sent out about six weeks into the term, include information about SOAP status, and if students are in non-clear categories, suggestions for improvement and intervention. The letters are meant as an "early warning" system so that students are alerted about impending academic problems in time to correct the situation.

Academic Alert was implemented in 1978, along with SOAP. Within the first three years, a random telephone poll indicated that 93% of the students appreciated the letters (Anandam, 1981). Over this same three-year period,

> The percentage of students performing satisfactorily at the middle of a term has increased from 45 to 52 percent. While this statistic cannot be claimed as evidence for the effectiveness of the Academic Alert and Advisement system *per se*, it does point to the overall goal of the system to prompt the students to perform better by alerting them early enough to be useful (Anandam, 1981, p. 1).

Surveys by the 1984 self-study group indicated that the letters had a positive effect on student academic performance, and students, faculty, and administrators strongly agreed that "it is important to notify students by mid-term if the student's academic performance is not satisfactory" (Ossip, 1984, p. 51). In fact, many students requested that Academic Alert letters be sent out during the shorter spring and summer terms as well. In the 1984 survey, 37% of both spring and fall students said they improved their performance as a result of receiving an Academic Alert letter. However, these percentages were not as low as they appear because 25% of all students surveyed were in their first term and had never received a letter. Also included were many students who received all satisfactory ratings and had no need to improve performance (Ossip, 1984).

The great majority of faculty, staff, and students understood the purpose of Academic Alert letters, and all agreed that Miami-Dade should continue to spend money to maintain the system, with support ranging from 60% of the administrators and staff to 77% of the fall students.

The biggest problem that the self-study committee found with Academic Alert was inconsistent standards. Even within a campus, professors sent out unsatisfactory notices for different levels of performance and different numbers of absences. In a related matter, students also asked that the letters identify superior performance; as the system stands, the term "satisfactory" may be used to describe performance ranging from A to D. Students would prefer to see more positive reinforcement of excellent work. The committee's first recommendation was to establish a college-wide standard for "not satisfactory" performance and to use a clear set of terms, such as letter grades, so that students have feedback that is more specific than "satisfactory" and "nonsatisfactory" (Ossip, 1984).

Advisement and Graduation Information System (AGIS)

AGIS is the system of computerized reports that provide complete information to Miami-Dade students about their progress through the program they have selected. AGIS reports show assessment scores, courses completed, courses necessary for completion of a degree or program, and courses necessary for smooth transfer to the State University System or a private college. These reports are arranged with the courses taken lined up against the courses needed, rather than being arranged in the usual chronological order by term, so that students can easily see what they need to take next in order to complete their requirements.

"If there is a universal criticism of colleges and universities across the country, it is probably the lack of sophistication and preciseness in the academic advisement process" (Harper, Herrig, Kelly, & Schinoff, 1981, p. 1). Basically the problem is too many students, too few advisors, and too little information available. AGIS helps solve this problem by providing the information quickly and completely. Thus the advisor can easily see what a student needs to take next, and costly errors are more easily avoided. All faculty members are now part of the advisement process, and all students must be advised by a faculty member. Miami-Dade estimates that AGIS saves the college $100,000 a year in salaries to professional staff for work checking graduation requirements, prerequisites for courses, and other information.

The 1984 self-study survey on AGIS revealed that 83% to 90% of the respondents thought the AGIS system effectively provided information about courses required for graduation. In fact, when the surveyors asked administrators and staff what single major change had had the most positive impact on the college in the last ten years, more of them named AGIS than any other change. The consensus is that AGIS is a reform that provides much useful, well-organized, necessary information, and that the system should remain in place.

The self-study committee recommended some changes in the format and language of the AGIS reports, and in the fall of 1986 Miami-Dade will institute AGIS II, a revised version of the computer-generated student report. This new report system has several "new and improved" features.

> The first, the actual course sequencing report, lists suggested and required courses in several columns. Based upon a student's major, test scores, and university of choice, the English sequence is indicated in the first column, the Math sequence in the second column, the General Education core in the third column, and if a transfer student, the General Education distribution courses, electives, and Physical Education requirements in remaining columns (Harper & Schinoff, 1985, p. 1).

Other variations exist for students working toward A.S. degrees or certificates. "As students complete courses, the computer indicates the grade the student received in the course. If currently enrolled the computer places an asterisk next to the course and if preregistered for a future term a plus sign" (Harper & Schinoff, 1985, p. 2).

Other features of AGIS II reports include a list of the prerequisites and co-requisites the student is required to take, with computer "holds" which prevent a student from registering inappropriately for advanced courses. A third feature is a list of holds that the student will encounter when attempting to register, so the student does not waste time standing in line to sign up for a course for which he is ineligible. Finally, the report indicates career information based upon the student's major, some general and some specific. (See Figure 7.)

THE RESULTS

Ultimately, students leave Miami-Dade. Some of them leave without completing a program or degree, but others finish their programs, write

CLAST successfully, and get their degrees. An effective way to measure outcomes is to look at the results of CLAST and at the numbers of students who earn degrees and are graduated.

CLAST Results

"Passing" the CLAST is defined as scoring above a specified "cut" score on either three or four of the four subtests. Students must pass all four subtests in order to get an A.A. degree. They must pass three of the four in order to continue their education in the State University System (SUS). The minimum scores that define "passing" on each subtest will rise in 1986 and again in 1989.

More Miami-Dade students have passed the CLAST each year it has been given. In fall 1983, 13.3% passed zero, one, or two subtests, while 24% passed three and 62.7% passed all four. In fall 1984, 8.6%

Sample AGIS Report

DATE PRINTED: 12/20/84	MIAMI-DADE COMMUNITY COLLEGE ADVISEMENT AND GRADUATION INFORMATION SYSTEM ASSOCIATE IN ARTS DEGREE	PAGE 1 OF 3

COURSE SEQUENCING - SOUTH CAMPUS

STUDENT NAME: JOHN CHARLES STUDENT   STUDENT NUMBER: 1234567

PROGRAM OF STUDY: 04 BUSINESS ADMINISTRATION

TRANSFER OBJECTIVE: FLORIDA STATE UNIVERSITY	BASIC SKILLS CGP SCORES	READ 13	WRITE 10	COMP 12	ALG 00	DATE 09/02/84

ENGLISH REQUIREMENT (15 CREDITS) FN COURSE GR CR	MATHEMATICS REQUIREMENT (12 CREDITS) FN COURSE GR CR	GENERAL EDUCATION CORE REQUIREMENT (12 CREDITS) FN COURSE GR CR	GENERAL EDUCATION DISTRIBUTION REQUIREMENT (9 CREDITS) FN COURSE GR CR	ELECTIVES (21 CREDITS) FN COURSE GR CR	PHYSICAL EDUCATION REQUIREMENT (2 CREDITS) FN COURSE GR CR
ENG0007 S 3.0 1 REA1105 * 3.0 2 ENG1101 3.0 #ENG1102 3.0 #ENG2301 3.0	MAT0003 S 3.0 MAT1024 A 3.0 ------------- MATHEMATICS DISTRIBUTION 3.0 MAC1102 C 3.0 ------------- MGF1113 * 3.0	3 HUM1020 B 3.0 3 PSC1515 3.0 3 PSY1000 * 3.0 3 SS11120 C 3.0	HUMANITIES DISTRIBUTION 3.0 ARH1000 C 3.0 4 NATURAL SCIENCE DISTRIBUTION 3.0 SOCIAL SCIENCE DISTRIBUTION 3.0 PSY2012 C 3.0	THE FOLLOWING COURSES ARE REQUIRED FOR TRANSFER: 8#ACG2001 3.0 #ACG2011 3.0 7 COC1312C 3.0 COP1110 3.0 #ECO2013 3.0 #ECO2023 3.0 #MAC1132 3.0 #MAC1142 3.0 #MAC2233 3.0 6#QMB2100 3.0 6 STA2014 C 3.0 THE FOLLOWING COURSES ARE SUGGESTED FOR TRANSFER: #ACG2071 3.0 ELECTIVE CREDITS TAKEN FROM COURSES NOT IN ABOVE LIST: 18.0 CREDIT REQUIREMENTS MET-ALL COURSES RECOMMENDED	5 HLP1010 3.0 OR TWO ONE-CREDIT PHYSICAL EDUCATION ACTIVITY COURSES
CREDITS REQUIRED TO COMPLETE THIS COLUMN: 9.0	CREDIT REQUIREMENTS MET	CREDITS REQUIRED TO COMPLETE THIS COLUMN: 3.0	CREDITS REQUIRED TO COMPLETE THIS COLUMN: 3.0	OR SUGGESTED FOR TRANSFER HAVE NOT BEEN TAKEN	CREDITS REQUIRED TO COMPLETE THIS COLUMN: 2.0

■FIGURE 7

passed only zero, one, or two, but the number of passers increased to 16% for three subtests and 75.4% for all four. In spring 1985, an impressive 87.5% passed all four subtests. These spring 1985 scores are significantly higher than those for previous years. In a memorandum to several internal committees, Dr. Marcia Belcher of Miami-Dade's Office of Institutional Research pointed out that basic skills and English proficiency of entering students are closely related to CLAST scores. She posed the possibility that the CLAST scores were higher because the entering scores were higher. However, research did not bear her out. The current test takers are no different in these two areas from previous test takers. "This finding indicates that changes wrought by the institution probably have had an impact on increasing CLAST scores" (Belcher, 1985c, p. 1).

The spring 1985 CLAST examination produced some impressive results for Miami-Dade. The 87.5% of Miami-Dade students who passed all four subtests represented a better performance than that of students at the local universities, both of which admit only well-qualified students. The college continued to make exceptional progress on the math subtest, scoring above the state average in spite of different makeup of the student body. (For example, Miami-Dade's group included 58% of all Hispanics in Florida who took the test.) Not only did the group as a whole score above the state average, but also each sub-group—male, female, white, black, Hispanic, and foreign—scored above the state average. And, as usual, about 30% of those who were successful on the 1985 CLAST were students who originally had deficiencies and therefore would not have been admitted to the university system.

A community college has twin responsibilities regarding students who want to continue their education in a university or other four-year school. One is to provide a parallel education for the students who are already proficient in basic skills. These students were eligible to enter the SUS as freshmen, and they expect to receive an education at Miami-Dade that is comparable to what they would have received in the SUS. The other responsibility, of course, is to take students deficient in one or more basic skills at the time of entry into Miami-Dade and help them become proficient so that they can enter the SUS when they leave Miami-Dade, even though they were ineligible as freshmen.

Miami-Dade has done well for both groups. One study followed the first-time-in-college freshmen for the fall of 1981 through the CLAST writing for fall 1984 (Belcher & Losak, 1985). Students who were "SUS eligible" and passed all three CGP assessment tests at entry did as well as or better than students actually enrolled in the SUS. In the fall 1983 CLAST administration, Miami-Dade students out-performed students at eight out of nine universities in the system; in fall 1984, they outperformed those at all but three. Miami-Dade students performed similarly to SUS students not only overall, but also on each of the subtests. In reading, 97.7% of the Miami-Dade students passed, compared to 97.1% of the SUS students. In writing, 97.3% of Miami-Dade students passed, compared to 97.6% of the SUS students. The same percentage (98.2%) of both groups passed computation. On the essay, 95.5% of the Miami-Dade students passed, compared to 92.7% of the SUS students. From these scores, it is clear that "the academically well-prepared student who enrolls at Miami-Dade is not academically handicapped by attending a community college in terms of future CLAST performance" (Belcher & Losak, 1985, p. 3).

In this same study, 688 students who were not eligible for the SUS as entering freshmen passed either three or four CLAST subtests and thus became eligible for entry. These 688 students represented 14% of the 4924 students who fell below the cut scores in one or more areas when they entered in 1981. But these 688 students also indicate that the community college experience enables them to continue their education. In fact, 34% of the students graduating in 1983-84 took developmental courses in at least one area, and 4% (155 students) took such courses in all three areas. The door that might have been closed because of skills deficiencies was reopened by the open-door college.

There is a clear relationship between the basic skills entry level and CLAST. Students in the bottom quartile are particularly vulnerable to leaving and to doing poorly on CLAST. "Students who enter with deficiencies will be likely to exit with deficiencies, either because of withdrawal prior to the CLAST or failure at the time of the test" (Belcher, 1984a, p. 6). "As a competency based test, the CLAST does not make allowance for entering deficiencies in basic skills" (Belcher, 1985a, p. 1).

One problem for many Miami-Dade students is language. Over half Miami-Dade's students are not native speakers of English. When students pass the objective writing section but fail the essay,

> it is safe to say the large numbers of the students who were writing the exam were bilingual and perform in a more adequate manner on a multiple choice examination which assesses their knowledge of the English language than on an essay examination. This is a very common distinction and widely found

among persons who are learning a second language. From a practical standpoint, however, the students are going to be expected to perform adequately on the essay regardless of arguments that are presented regarding the dual language barrier (Losak, 1984a, pp. 2–3).

In spite of the low scores and language problems, college is not too late to remediate. In the 1981 study, almost a fourth of those who passed all four sections of CLAST were in the bottom quartile in at least one area when they started (Belcher, 1984a). In the June 1984 CLAST, 52% of those Miami-Dade students who passed all four subtests were not native speakers of English (McCabe, in press).

The problem is that Miami-Dade doesn't quite know how that remediation takes place. Whether students who succeed were remediated in developmental courses or in regular classes cannot be determined at this point. There are still many questions to be answered about developmental work. It is difficult to distinguish between the effects of developmental work and other factors, such as student motivation or attitude toward school. However, developmental work does not seem to have much long-term effect: "Indicators are . . . that effects have not been strong enough to be found when students must demonstrate their competence in basic skills on the CLAST several years after developmental work" (Belcher, 1985a, p. 9). Since only 14% of those entering 1981 freshmen who had a skills deficiency managed to take and pass CLAST, we must agree that "the role of remediation in breaking the link between entry level performance and exit level performance had been only partially effective" (Belcher, 1984a, p. 1). However, many students who entered in 1981 were still in the system and were not yet ready to take CLAST; thus the 14% figure is likely to rise as more students finish more coursework and take CLAST in later administrations. Miami-Dade students usually show excellent results in computation tests, where expertise in English is not a big factor, again supporting the premise that the native language of a student, as well as the quality of Miami-Dade courses, plays a major role in student success. For whatever reason, the 688 students who comprise the 14% did beat the odds, did improve their skills, and did pass CLAST. While we can't really determine what caused the success, we can certainly draw a relationship between the total instructional program and student performance. Many students who were initially underprepared received sufficient instruction at Miami-Dade to pass all four sections of CLAST and receive an A.A. degree (Losak, 1984c).

Grade Inflation

A problem that has emerged since the implementation of CLAST is grade inflation. Study after study has indicated that students can make relatively high grades at Miami-Dade and still fail one or more sections of CLAST. In one such study, 21% of a group of CLAST "failers" had GPAs of 3.0 or better (Belcher, 1984b, p. 3). Of 431 A.A. candidates who took CLAST in 1983 and who had a B average (3.00–4.00), 20.4% failed one or more subtests. This percentage represents 88 people; 78 failed essay, 8 computation, 3 writing, and 26 reading (Losak, 1984a). Nearly half (49%) Belcher's CLAST "failers" had an average grade of C. Math grades were not as inflated, "perhaps because the grading criteria are more distinct and involve attainment of one correct answer" (Belcher, 1984b, p. 3). However, Belcher concluded that "results have consistently shown that large numbers of students are being awarded passing grades in college-level courses which did not reflect achievement of the minimum basic skills required by CLAST" (Belcher, 1984b, p. 1). On the other hand, students who are not native speakers of English are more likely to be successful in a classroom environment than in a timed-test situation. As a result, students who earn good grades may do poorly on CLAST because of language problems. Therefore, low scores on CLAST may indicate grade inflation, but they may also indicate large numbers of non-native speakers who are unable to be highly successful in that particular kind of testing situation.

Grade inflation is not fair to students because it gives them an undeserved sense of accomplishment that can be shattered by a more realistic assessment (such as CLAST).

> Students transferring to universities from two-year colleges have typically experienced a decline as a group in grade point average. This has been interpreted as relating specifically to two factors. The first is referred to as transfer shock and is intended to include such variables as the adjustments attendant to moving away from home, relocating to a new social environment, and competing with students who are used to a fairly rigorous academic environment. The second reason attributed for the decline in grade point average is the generally inflated grades awarded by two-year college instructors (Losak, 1984a, p. 1).

Often GPAs drop from 2.7 or 2.8 to 2.2 or 2.3 in the first term at the university.

Losak also found that the modal grade on two of the four campuses at Miami-Dade was A. On three campuses there were more A's than C's. "These grade distributions reflect the continuance of grading practices that convey to students an unrealistic sense of accomplishment" (Losak, 1984a, p. 1). Losak concludes his report by stating that

> it is difficult to reconcile the fact that Miami-Dade is an open-door, two-year college with the fact that the modal grade awarded on two campuses is an A. One must be concerned regarding the primrose path students are finding themselves on as a result of their receipt of grades which reflect a knowledge that is not, in many instances, sufficiently substantive to be academically competitive, at least as measured by the CLAST (Losak, 1984a, p. 3).

However, as Dr. McCabe pointed out, when the "Drop" students are included, only about a quarter of the students make A's, with the distribution about even between A, B, C, D, F, and Drop. Although there may be too many A's, the distribution is not so badly skewed when all grades and Drops are considered.

The 1984 self-study addressed the problem of grade inflation in several parts of its findings. In "Volume II: Prescriptive Education," the editors expressed concern that Miami-Dade

> shares in the national concern of postsecondary educational institutions to maintain high standards of academic performance while also subscribing to an open-access philosophy. It should also be emphasized that challenging academic standards apply to developmental programs and to college-level courses equally (Garcia & Romanik, 1984, p. 57).

While exit-level testing is currently used in most developmental courses, the self-study committee recommended standardizing these tests and doing research to ensure that passing the exit-level test in a developmental course would lead to a high probability of making a C or better in a college-level course.

In another volume of the self-study, the Student Flow Subcommittee commented that "the figures [concerning the relationship between grades and CLAST] present significant implications concerning grade inflation and grading practices that convey an unrealistic sense of accomplishment for students" (Roberts, 1984, p. 152). The committee feels that required college-wide exit competency examinations for Communications, English Composition, and Advanced Composition might make grading less inflationary and allow grading practices to more accurately reflect the acquisition of basic skills in reading and compositions (Roberts, 1984, p. 153).

This recommendation echoes a suggestion from an empirical researcher that departmental, college-wide tests be given to ensure minimal competence for a grade of C. Miami-Dade has also developed its own mid-level CLAST, which is used as a preliminary check for competence after students have completed 30 hours. But Belcher pointed out, and the Self-Study Committee agreed, that "it is easier, however, to assess competence prior to awarding credit than it is to explain later that the credit was not a sufficient indication of competence and the student should be remediated" (Belcher, 1984b, p. 4).

It is clear that grades must be an accurate reflection of skills and performance. The Standards of Academic Progress are based on grades, but if the grades are unrealistically high, then the Standards, which are designed to ensure academic excellence, lose much of their value. However, the 1985 CLAST scores, with 87.5% of the students passing all four tests, would seem to indicate a closer correlation between grades and scores. Miami-Dade will, as usual, continue to monitor relationships between entry skills levels, developmental courses, grades, and CLAST, particularly since the self-study makes multiple recommendations in this area.

Completers

In the 25 years from its opening in 1960 to 1985, 100,000 students graduated from Miami-Dade Community College. The implementation of the reforms in the 1978–1982 period caused a slight drop in the number of graduates for one year, but the rates quickly went back up, often to levels exceeding those before the reforms.

> Forty-six percent of fulltime first-year-in-college students who entered the college in the Fall Term of 1977 were either graduated or still enrolled three years later. For a comparable 1981 group, 53% were either graduated or still enrolled three years later (Office of Institutional Research, 1984, p. 13).

In 1983–84, 5,159 students were awarded associate degrees or planned certificates. Of these, 3,860 students (74.5%) received an Associate in

Arts degree, 1,000 (19.4%) an Associate in Science degree, and 299 (5.8%) a Planned Certificate (Office of Institutional Research, 1984, p. 27).

Attrition rates at Miami-Dade do not, at first glance, look encouraging. Of those who failed all three of the CGP basic skills tests at entry in 1981, 70.7% left within three years with no degree. Of those who passed all three tests, 49.6% still left with no degree, 19.3% got a degree, and 21.3% were still enrolled three years later (Belcher & Losak, 1985, p. 4).

However, Dr. Robert McCabe, President of Miami-Dade, points out some explanatory factors:

> As few as one-third of the students begin full time with the objective of obtaining a degree. Others enter programs of two years or less for direct employment, and many are there for specialized objectives, including career-oriented or other personal goals. Such students may take one or two courses and feel they have achieved their objectives, but no measurement of program completion would reflect this (in press).

Many students at community colleges work, and many drop into and out of college. In an open-door institution, many must take developmental courses, which do not give college credit. The dual factors of job and developmental work often mean that students take less than a full credit load; thus they take longer to amass the total number of credits needed for a degree. For the 1984 Miami-Dade graduates, the mean term of attendance was eleven semesters; more than half had begun their college work more than five years earlier.

Many students pursuing a baccalaureate degree do not stay in a community college long enough to complete an A.A. degree. The A.A. has little importance to these students, and they frequently transfer to a university without completing the associate degree, often transferring, in fact, when they are near completion of the A.A. One out of every five students who are in the state university system has come through Miami-Dade; this is about twice the number who actually graduated from Miami-Dade.

What happens to students after they leave Miami-Dade? In a follow-up study of 1982–83 graduates, researchers were able to locate 3,179 (78%) of the 4,085 A.A. degree graduates. Of those 3,179, 59% were continuing their education and 41% were working. Eighty-three percent of those who received A.S. degrees or Planned Certificates were located. Of these 1,237 people, 7% were continuing their education and 92% were working (Office of Institutional Research, 1984, p. 29). Students who transfer to other institutions to continue their education after they graduate from Miami-Dade do very well. McCabe cites a Florida State Community College Coordinating Board study which shows no difference between transfer students and native university students in the number who are successful (have a GPA of 2.0 or higher) after one term of the junior year. In fact, 46.14% of the community college transfer students had a GPA of 3.0 or higher, compared with 45.49% of the native students (McCabe, in press).

It is clear that Miami-Dade students do follow specific directives about their flow through the college, and they do meet minimum academic standards. Yet they stay in school and graduate in greater numbers than before. Developmental courses may not be the answer to remediation, but something is, since Miami-Dade is able to send large numbers of students into the state university system every year who were academically underprepared when they started Miami-Dade. Grade inflation may be a problem, but the numbers of students passing all four CLAST tests have increased dramatically every year. Miami-Dade can claim that its "Systems for Success" are indeed successful.

C H A P T E R V

COLLEGE CLIMATE

Climate Pervades a System

Visiting someone's house generates a feeling about that house and the living that goes on inside. The house may look messy but feel comfortable and lived in or give a feeling of disorder, sloppiness, and confusion. The house may be neat and well-kept and give a sense of friendliness and order, or it may be so neat and formal you're afraid to sit down for fear you might mess something up. If you know the people in that house, you may have even more specific feelings. The house may have a feeling of strict discipline and even fear, or it may feel chaotic and unruly, or agreeable, cooperative, and comfortable. How the house looks and how the people who live in it behave with one another tell you things about the relationships and lifestyle of the house's inhabitants.

The same is true of organizations. Organizational theorists use the term "climate" to describe that intangible feeling or tone. Even though it is intangible, climate is a force that cannot be ignored. It is created by leaders in an organization who exert a strong influence on it, just as the "feeling" of a house is created by the leaders, usually adults, who strongly influence the behavior of others in the household. Climate can be felt by others in the organization (Litwin & Stringer, 1966), and it can be measured by using a scale and asking workers how they feel.

An organization may be described by workers as "a terrific place to work" or "a tough, demanding place where effort goes unrewarded" or "a bureaucratic nightmare." These statements refer to the climate, which research shows affects both performance and organizational growth (Litwin, Humphrey, & Wilson, 1978). When we mention climate, typically we are commenting on the extent to which we like or dislike a place and how comfortable we find it to advance our growth there. Achievement climates are correlated with productivity (Litwin & Stringer, 1968).

Forehand and Gilmer (1964) defined climate as "the set of characteristics that describe an organization and that: a) distinguish the organization from other organizations, b) are relatively enduring over time, and c) influence the behavior of people in the organization" (p. 362). Gellerman (1959) adds that organizational climate develops as a result of management styles by "persons who count." Campbell, Dunnette, Lawler, & Weick (1970) define it as "a set of attributes specific to

95

a particular organization that may be induced from the way the organization deals with its members and its environment" (p. 390). Likert (1967) describes climate as causal variables such as structure, objectives, supervisory practices, and the like that interact with personality to produce perceptions. All these definitions generate parameters necessary to study the nebulous concept of climate.

Generally, we can conclude that the experts in climate research agree on several commonalities: that climate is defined through the perceptions of its members, that it influences their behaviors through leadership and management styles, and that it sets an organization apart from others like it, almost as personality does with people (Steers, 1977).

Organizational Climate As Part of a System

A system functions as a result of three factors which determine the outcomes of the organization. The first is the system used by the institution to manage in general; the second is the way the individual administrator makes decisions or applies that system; and the third is the values of the employees in that department (Litwin et al., 1978). The second and third chapters of this book describe in some detail the system of management President McCabe has designed to meet the needs of his college in his community. Individual administrators at Miami-Dade are given latitude in using their own styles of leadership to their best advantage and to meet the specific needs of their campuses and their situations. Although we did not chronicle those responses in terms of climate, we describe what we feel were the characteristics shared by these excellent administrators in the leadership chapter. The third factor, departmental values, was not examined in this study, but would suggest a need for some adaptation of the system to fit "local" departmental situations.

We have indications that the employees of the Miami-Dade Community College feel they have a very positive climate. In fact, on our instrument, which has now been used by other "good" community colleges, mean responses of employees of Miami-Dade were on the average almost a full point above the mean responses of other colleges on our seven-point scale (Baker, 1985).

Research Methodology

The Institutional Climate Survey was sent to a total of 731 Miami-Dade employees comprising four groups: faculty, line administrators, and classified or support staff. A random sample was selected of approximately one-third of each group from each campus. As a result, 36 line administrators, 270 faculty, 121 staff administrators, and 304 classified employees received the climate survey. Respondents were asked to complete and return the survey to the Office of Institutional Research at Miami-Dade within a week of receiving the form. Two hundred and sixty employees returned the survey for a combined return rate of 35%. The survey forms were color-coded for the four different groups so that their answers could be distinguished. Only administrators whose responsibilities included clear supervision activities were represented in the line administrative sample. Similarly, a number of employees who are typically grouped as classified were, on the basis of their responsibilities at the college, combined with the staff administrative group. Therefore, the classified employee group represented individuals whose responsibilities were generally clerical/secretarial or non-technical in nature. Represented in the faculty group were not only full-time teachers but also individuals on full-time faculty contracts but not necessarily engaged in teaching, such as counselors and librarians.

The results of these surveys were then tabulated and ratings on each item were determined by the mean for each group. We will be reporting these four means per item in our discussion of the results of the climate survey in this chapter.

Descriptors of Climate

An assumption held by many researchers is that a small number of factors can be used to describe organizational climate. Campbell et al. (1970) discovered four common dimensions in different scales: (1) individual autonomy, (2) degree of structure imposed on the situation, (3) reward orientation, and (4) consideration, warmth, and support. Moos (1973) found three types of dimensions which characterize and differentiate climates: (1) relationship dimensions measure the degree to which individuals are involved in the environment and support and help one another; (2) personal development dimensions measure the way personal development and self-enhancement occur in a specific climate; and (3) system maintenance and change dimensions describe the order, organization, control, and clarity. Work pressure and innovation are also related to morale and coping behaviors under this dimension. Taylor and Bowers (1972) simplified Likert's list of organizational processes to distill four identifiable factors of climate: decision making, motivation, communication, and human resources primacy.

Dimensions of Climate

We chose Likert's own list of organizational processes to analyze the climate at Miami-Dade Community College. We adapted the Likert instrument (1967) on organizational characteristics to investigate five areas that describe climate variables: leadership, motivation, communication, and decision making, adding the category "rewards" to incorporate another aspect of climate which we felt, from the literature, was paramount in studying excellence in colleges. Our overall findings indicate that the four groups generally responded in a similar pattern; that is, the line administrators were most positive in their responses, followed by staff administrators, classified staff, and faculty. Most organizational analysts attribute this pattern to the degree these groups feel they are distant from variables related to controlling the institution.

Likert's Management Systems

Rensis Likert divided organizations into four management types. System 1 operates along the lines of McGregor's Theory X, assuming that subordinates are ordered about by leadership and are controlled by threats and punishment. System 2 is slightly better with some input by employees, but generally a more kindly "master-servant" relationship. System 3 involves more exchange, but the levels are still distinct, with management holding the key decision-making role. System 4 is similar to a Theory Y management system based on the assumption that employees are trustworthy, are interested in doing their best to attain institution goals, and are active in decision making with leaders who value their input. On the seven-point scale we will be using to report the results of our data, almost every score was in the System 3 or 4 range. (Scores of 4 to 5.5 fall in the System 3 range; scores of 5.5 to 7 in System 4.)

Leadership

Because organizations which have frequent turnover in leadership are not able to maintain continuity or to influence consistently the behaviors of members, they usually are not able to establish a strong climate. Climate is solidified by the longevity and power of its leadership. President McCabe is a strong leader who has been able to mold a "cultural" identity among his employees. One of the values Dr. McCabe cherishes is excellence in coworkers, and the group of talented administrators he has gathered around him attests to his belief that excellence cannot be achieved alone. These campus leaders add significantly to the successful climate of Miami-Dade Community College.

The results of the leadership section of the Institutional Climate Survey are listed in Figure 8. Both groups of administrators and the classified staff rate all items in this category well above the scale average of four. All groups scored in the System 4 range on the item "shows confidence in staff." Clearly all four groups feel that the climate of Miami-Dade is supportive on this item and that there is a shared confidence and trust expressed by administration about faculty and staff. In terms of "approachability" or the feeling that faculty and staff can talk things over with administration, administrators responded in the System 4 range, and faculty and classified staff in the System 3 range. Likert himself does not discriminate clearly between these two ranges; employees are either rather free (System 3) or very free (System 4) to discuss their jobs with their superiors. The faculty indicated that although they felt the climate at Miami-Dade was generally high, it was not exceptional on seeking and using faculty ideas, assistance in improvement of teaching and supportive behavior toward faculty. However, the difference between a System 3 or System 4 response lies in how close the response is to the "always" end of the scale. Obviously, many people feel "always" is a rare phenomenon; therefore, it is not surprising that the scores are not higher on these three items. The classified staff agreed on a System 3 assessment of seeking and using faculty ideas, but rated the other two in the System 4 range, just as the administrative groups did. Although faculty scores are lower, none of the scores was below a System 3 rating.

Decision Making

Although leadership is an important component of climate, it is not climate. In a study distinguishing between leadership and organizational climate, Franklin (1975a) supports Likert (1961, 1967), Taylor & Bowers (1972) and Bowers (1973) by suggesting that group process and climate can be viewed as outcome measures, which do in fact influence the functioning of the organization. Bowers (1973) asserts that a positive organizational climate is critical to improving the supportiveness and goal orientation of supervisors. Since we know that leadership sets the tone of an organization, this almost sounds like a "chicken or the egg" dilemma; does climate or leadership begin the cycle? We

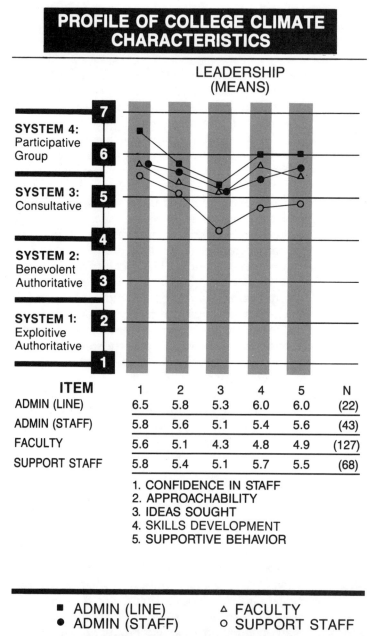

PROFILE OF COLLEGE CLIMATE CHARACTERISTICS

LEADERSHIP (MEANS)

SYSTEM 4: Participative Group

SYSTEM 3: Consultative

SYSTEM 2: Benevolent Authoritative

SYSTEM 1: Exploitive Authoritative

ITEM	1	2	3	4	5	N
ADMIN (LINE)	6.5	5.8	5.3	6.0	6.0	(22)
ADMIN (STAFF)	5.8	5.6	5.1	5.4	5.6	(43)
FACULTY	5.6	5.1	4.3	4.8	4.9	(127)
SUPPORT STAFF	5.8	5.4	5.1	5.7	5.5	(68)

1. CONFIDENCE IN STAFF
2. APPROACHABILITY
3. IDEAS SOUGHT
4. SKILLS DEVELOPMENT
5. SUPPORTIVE BEHAVIOR

■ ADMIN (LINE) △ FACULTY
● ADMIN (STAFF) ○ SUPPORT STAFF

FIGURE 8

have interpreted Franklin and Bowers' work to mean that shared deci-sion making creates a leadership influence at lower levels and that these leaders are creating the climate while also being influenced by upper echelon leaders.

Although the overall climate findings were very positive, one of the items which was scored lower by all groups was in the decision-making area (see Figure 9). We found that the line administrators rated their involvement in decision making about the work environment and in decisions affecting the quality of their work in the System 4 range. Staff administrators gave slightly less positive marks to being involved in decision making that affects their work environment and higher marks to involvement in decisions about the quality of their work. Faculty and classified staff gave mostly System 3 ratings to these two items.

Relatively low ratings were given to the question on the extent to which the respondents were involved in establishing college goals. Two of the four groups responded with a less than average (System 2) in-volvement with goal setting, and all four groups expressed a less positive response to this item than to previous ones. We offer the observation of Miami-Dade master teacher, Alice Huff:

> Administrators feel faculty are included as representatives on decision-making councils, so they perceive faculty as included. Individual faculty members are not on the councils, so see themselves as not having direct participation. However, some of these duties are the responsibility of the Board of Trustees, and are therefore outside the realm of others in the organization.

Goal-setting may be an example of a topic that often is decided by board policy, and for this reason we suggest that its inclusion under this section be reconsidered before the climate instrument is used again.

Motivation

One of the components of motivation is innovation, since it is gener-ally fostered through administrative support of faculty. Forehand (1968) found that innovation was present more often in autonomy-centered organizations than in rules-centered organizations. Fredericksen, Jensen, and Beaton (1972) found restrictive rules were repressive in a production area requiring creativity and interaction. Jones and James (1977) found nonroutine, complex technology significantly related to organizational

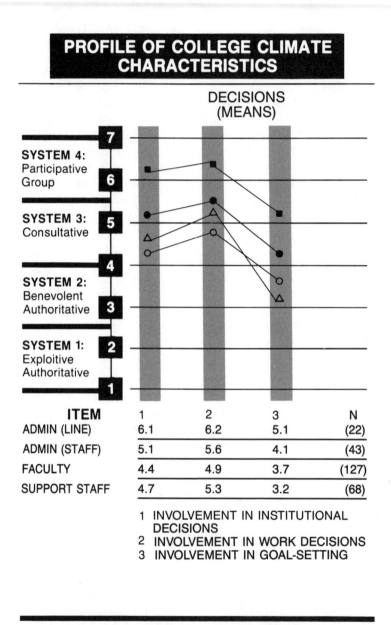

PROFILE OF COLLEGE CLIMATE CHARACTERISTICS

DECISIONS
(MEANS)

7

SYSTEM 4:
Participative
Group

6

SYSTEM 3:
Consultative

5

4

SYSTEM 2:
Benevolent
Authoritative

3

SYSTEM 1:
Exploitive
Authoritative

2

1

ITEM	1	2	3	N
ADMIN (LINE)	6.1	6.2	5.1	(22)
ADMIN (STAFF)	5.1	5.6	4.1	(43)
FACULTY	4.4	4.9	3.7	(127)
SUPPORT STAFF	4.7	5.3	3.2	(68)

1 INVOLVEMENT IN INSTITUTIONAL
  DECISIONS
2 INVOLVEMENT IN WORK DECISIONS
3 INVOLVEMENT IN GOAL-SETTING

■ ADMIN (LINE)   △ FACULTY
● ADMIN (STAFF)   ○ SUPPORT STAFF

■FIGURE 9

climate measures of cooperation, friendliness, and warmth. Certainly a college setting such as Miami-Dade would be described as nonroutine and complex, since the excellent teaching which is one product acts as an input for another product, student achievement.

According to Payne and Pugh (1976), in their study of climate related to organizational size, the hypothesis that large organizations are more bureaucratic and encourage conformity, suspicion, and little commitment to work has not been borne out. Instead, they found that organizational size affects the way work is done. The smaller the institution, the more the technology (in this case teaching methods) influences the structure of the organization. In other words, we can expect to find more support for innovation in a large institution, which is exactly what we found at Miami-Dade.

Rothman's study of affluence and innovation (1974) revealed several findings that are relevant to colleges. Larger organizations with more resources tend to be more innovative and use uncommitted resources for innovative advances; smaller organizations expend less for innovation but implement to a greater degree what they do create. If an organization chooses to emphasize low costs and quantity rather than quality, it will be less innovative.

Results in this section show exceptionally high enthusiasm for the current climate at Miami-Dade. We interpret this to mean that employees feel motivation factors are strong (see Figure 10). Both administrative groups and classified staff report that they find the extent to which innovative ideas and professional development are supported is exceptionally high. Faculty at Miami-Dade also report that they feel well-supported in their innovative efforts and their professional development by administrative personnel. In discussing freedom to innovate, Professor Roslyn Reich told us,

> the free academic climate my chairperson, Elizabeth Forrester, has created over the past 15 years enables me to structure my course curriculum and time outside of the classroom in a most creative manner. Under those conditions, I could go on teaching at MDCC indefinitely.

We see tremendous agreement and commitment to the college's mission. All four groups are exceptionally positive in their response to this item. A strong System 4 management style is shown here.

A little less agreement surrounds cooperation across departments, with almost all groups reporting at the System 3 level. We would caution that faculty who have less daily interaction outside their own

PROFILE OF COLLEGE CLIMATE CHARACTERISTICS

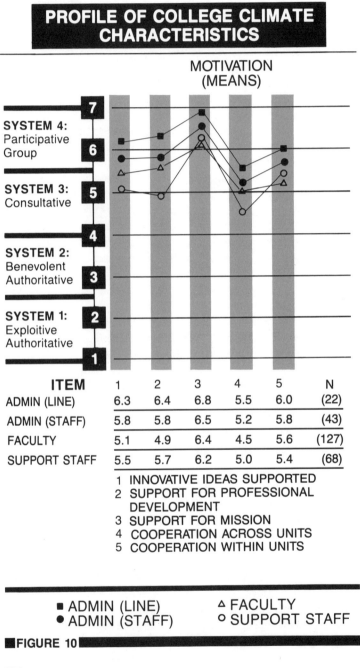

MOTIVATION
(MEANS)

ITEM	1	2	3	4	5	N
ADMIN (LINE)	6.3	6.4	6.8	5.5	6.0	(22)
ADMIN (STAFF)	5.8	5.8	6.5	5.2	5.8	(43)
FACULTY	5.1	4.9	6.4	4.5	5.6	(127)
SUPPORT STAFF	5.5	5.7	6.2	5.0	5.4	(68)

1 INNOVATIVE IDEAS SUPPORTED
2 SUPPORT FOR PROFESSIONAL
  DEVELOPMENT
3 SUPPORT FOR MISSION
4 COOPERATION ACROSS UNITS
5 COOPERATION WITHIN UNITS

SYSTEM 4: Participative Group
SYSTEM 3: Consultative
SYSTEM 2: Benevolent Authoritative
SYSTEM 1: Exploitive Authoritative

■ ADMIN (LINE)   △ FACULTY
● ADMIN (STAFF)   ○ SUPPORT STAFF

■FIGURE 10■

104

department may also not feel the need for more cooperation; they do feel more positive about the interactions within their own departments, as do the other three groups surveyed. On this item we see their responses nearing all System 4 responses. These are extremely high scores for all four groups, with great consensus around a positive motivational climate.

Communication

Likert (1967) describes the flow of information in a System 4 organization as occurring between both individuals and groups. Much exchange is necessary to attain departmental and college goals. Members take responsibility to communicate relevant information and to initiate an information flow both upward and across the structure. Adequate and accurate information is available to ensure good decision making. All of this appears to line administrators to be occurring, as demonstrated by their collective responses to the items in this category shown in Figure 11.

Although the importance of strategic information is more accentuated for administrators than for faculty, good information is always necessary to make good decisions. As a result, several items were included to address this issue. Our findings confirm that Miami-Dade has an exceptional information network that is highly regarded by all four groups in the survey. Staff administrators, classified staff, and faculty also agree that there is much communication which is often accepted but is not as often questioned or discussed. Results were solidly favorable, although faculty did trail the other groups when queried about the willingness of administrators to share information and, conversely, about their own acceptance of such information.

Rewards

Many researchers think that managerial personnel contribute more to climate than do others in most organizations:

> If the climate is one which rewards and supports the display of individual differences, people in the same system will not behave similarly. Further, because satisfaction is a personal evaluation of a system's practices and procedures, people in the system will tend to agree less on their satisfaction than on their description of the system's climate (Schneider, 1975, p. 479).

PROFILE OF COLLEGE CLIMATE CHARACTERISTICS

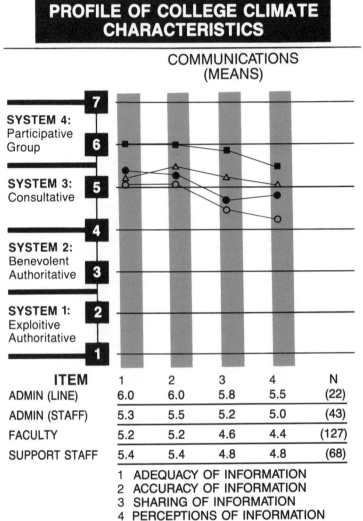

COMMUNICATIONS (MEANS)

SYSTEM 4: Participative Group

SYSTEM 3: Consultative

SYSTEM 2: Benevolent Authoritative

SYSTEM 1: Exploitive Authoritative

ITEM	1	2	3	4	N
ADMIN (LINE)	6.0	6.0	5.8	5.5	(22)
ADMIN (STAFF)	5.3	5.5	5.2	5.0	(43)
FACULTY	5.2	5.2	4.6	4.4	(127)
SUPPORT STAFF	5.4	5.4	4.8	4.8	(68)

1 ADEQUACY OF INFORMATION
2 ACCURACY OF INFORMATION
3 SHARING OF INFORMATION
4 PERCEPTIONS OF INFORMATION
  QUALITY

■ ADMIN (LINE)   △ FACULTY
● ADMIN (STAFF)   ○ SUPPORT STAFF

■FIGURE 11

Schneider and Snyder (1975) dispelled the notion that climate was equal to satisfaction. In their study neither climate nor satisfaction is strongly correlated with production data, but satisfaction, not climate, did correlate with turnover data. Litwin and Stringer (1968) found that businesses with "achievement climates" were significantly more productive and innovative than organizations with either power or affiliation climates. This study seems to support the Fredericksen notion that the focus of the organizational climate when made explicit and consistent exerts a positive influence.

In our adaptation of the Likert instrument, we added the category "rewards" to measure an aspect of satisfaction suggested by other researchers in the field, such as Forehand and Gilmer (1964). Our results are reported in Figure 12. Enormous agreement is shown about the extent to which college programs meet the needs of students. A definite System 4 style is indicated here by all groups. Again most groups agreed that they felt generally positive about the rewards offered at Miami-Dade; however, faculty felt that teaching excellence was not as well rewarded as perhaps it could be. All except the line administrators also felt that their individual performances were rewarded to only an average degree; faculty indicated a response slightly below average.

Overall Findings and Conclusions

On the first overall question concerning the effectiveness of administration's efforts to manage and enhance teaching quality in the college, we find a split between System 4 and System 3 responses (see Figure 13). This time, the line administrators and the classified staff feel a superb job is being done. Staff administrators and faculty are a little more conservative in their response, yet still very positive. The second overall item asks to what extent the climate created on the respondent's campus is conducive to excellent performance. The results are generally more positive, although again we are seeing a predominantly System 3 management style. Again, we remind readers that this is a composite of responses from a random sample of all Miami-Dade personnel; the true heartbeat of the institution is being illustrated here, not just the opinions of the leaders.

It is extremely important to remember that a "regression to the mean" mentality is easy to slip into as we interpret these data. In other words, it is easy to begin to talk about a score of 4.5 as a low mark, when in fact it is a high mark. On some of the items, the responses were so heavily positive that in comparison, others seem almost negative.

107

PROFILE OF COLLEGE CLIMATE CHARACTERISTICS

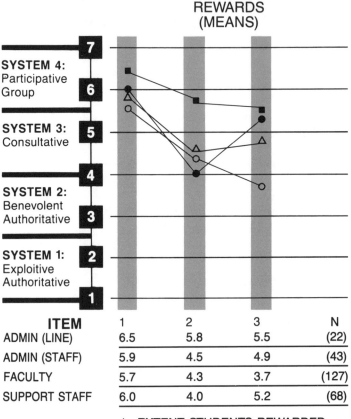

REWARDS
(MEANS)

SYSTEM 4:
Participative
Group

SYSTEM 3:
Consultative

SYSTEM 2:
Benevolent
Authoritative

SYSTEM 1:
Exploitive
Authoritative

ITEM	1	2	3	N
ADMIN (LINE)	6.5	5.8	5.5	(22)
ADMIN (STAFF)	5.9	4.5	4.9	(43)
FACULTY	5.7	4.3	3.7	(127)
SUPPORT STAFF	6.0	4.0	5.2	(68)

1 EXTENT STUDENTS REWARDED
2 PERSONAL PERFORMANCE
   REWARDED
3 EXCELLENT TEACHING REWARDED

■ ADMIN (LINE)   △ FACULTY
● ADMIN (STAFF)   ○ SUPPORT STAFF

■FIGURE 12■

PROFILE OF COLLEGE CLIMATE CHARACTERISTICS

OVERALL CLIMATE

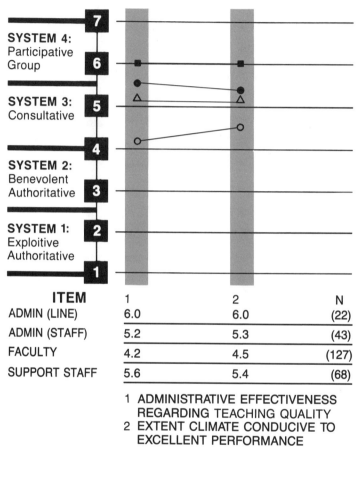

ITEM	1	2	N
ADMIN (LINE)	6.0	6.0	(22)
ADMIN (STAFF)	5.2	5.3	(43)
FACULTY	4.2	4.5	(127)
SUPPORT STAFF	5.6	5.4	(68)

1 ADMINISTRATIVE EFFECTIVENESS REGARDING TEACHING QUALITY
2 EXTENT CLIMATE CONDUCIVE TO EXCELLENT PERFORMANCE

■ ADMIN (LINE)   △ FACULTY
● ADMIN (STAFF)   ○ SUPPORT STAFF

■FIGURE 13■

We must not fall into this trap. These are extremely high responses for a random sample of all groups of employees to give, and an overall climate of System 3 is definitely something for a college to be proud of. System 4 is a style most likely to occur in a highly organic, decentralized, innovative, and professional organization. This is not to say colleges should not try to achieve a System 4 management style, but that each management style is appropriate to different organizations at different stages of growth and development, and Miami-Dade is now in a high System 3 stage.

Likert would argue that a System 4 management style leads to more productivity; perhaps as Miami-Dade continues to evolve it will show even higher levels of student achievement, the goal of any excellent college. We believe that our research of excellence of climate factors is helpful to other researchers, and to college leaders interested in improving the climate of their institutions.

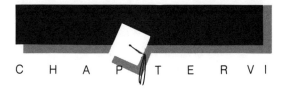

C H A P T E R VI

COMMUNITY COLLEGE LEADERSHIP

I nvestigating the leadership at Miami-Dade Community College was an extremely important aspect of our study. One way to discover what comprises effective leadership is to examine what the leaders of a successful organization do. Consequently, we observed the actions, motivations, and values of administrators representing the best at Miami-Dade. Altogether we surveyed and interviewed twenty-five administrators. The eight members of the executive management team—president, central staff vice presidents, and campus vice presidents—composed one group. The second group consisted of deans, associate deans, and one director who were selected by peers and faculty as among the best leaders in the college (members of the executive management team were excluded from the college-wide selection process). Listed below are the Miami-Dade administrators who participated in our study of leadership excellence:

Executive Management Team

Daniel Gill, Board Chairman
Robert McCabe, President
Duane Hansen, Vice President, Administration, District
Roy Phillips, Vice President, Public Information, District
Piedad Robertson, Vice President, Education, District
Lester Brookner, Vice President, Business Affairs, District
Terrence Kelly, Vice President, North Campus
William Stokes, Vice President, South Campus
Elizabeth Lundgren, Vice President, Medical Center Campus

Administrators selected for outstanding performance
North Campus

Daniel Derrico, Dean for Administration
Blanca Gonzalez, Chairperson, Accounting/Business
    Administration
Jeffrey Lukenbill, District Dean, Academic Affairs (now Dean,
    Academic Affairs, North Campus)
Wayne Silver, Associate Dean, Communication

113

South Campus
Jon Alexiou, Associate Dean, Social Science (now Vice President of Academic Affairs, District)
James Harvey, Associate Dean, Physical Education
Jane MacDonald, Associate Dean, Natural Sciences
Thomas McKitterick, Dean, Academic Affairs
Margaret Pelton, Associate Dean, Academic Affairs
Richard Schinoff, Dean of Student Services

Wolfson Campus
Yillian Coppolechia, Associate Dean for Bilingual Studies
Suzanne Richter, Dean of Instruction
Kathleen Sigler, Dean for Administration

Medical Center Campus
George Hedgespeth, Dean for Administration
Jeanne Stark, Dean, Nursing Education

District
Kamala Anandam, Director, Computer-Based Instructional
. Development and Research
John Losak, Dean, Institutional Research

During our study, we wanted to discover specific leadership attributes and other forces at work which appear to be linked to the successes at Miami-Dade. Our goal was to delineate the qualities leaders need to acquire and to develop in order to foster the cooperation necessary among all employees for creating the positive institutional climate and the effective instructional programs and systems at Miami-Dade.

To accomplish this goal, we asked each subject to complete a lengthy, open-ended questionnaire and to grant us an hour-long interview employing McClelland's (1978) Behavior Event Interview Technique (BEIT). The BEIT asks subjects, in response to specific questions, to describe critical incidents occurring in the course of their work. In describing an event which has resulted in personal change or development, the narrator reveals attitudes, values, skills, and qualities which characterize his or her actions. McClelland's method involves a coding procedure which factors out striking attributes and commonalities appearing in the narrative data. Beginning with a conceptual model adopted from Brown's *Leadership Vitality*, we built from that framework and from the data of our Model of Situational Leadership (see Figure 14).

From our many interviews, discussions, and dialogues with President McCabe, we have found ample support for the conclusion drawn by the Commission on Strengthening Presidential Leadership led by Clark Kerr that *Presidents Make a Difference* (1984). Our study takes the statement in the title of that report a step further by concluding that an even greater difference is made when a strong president is supported by an administrative team with similar convictions and qualities. While our competency model is largely characteristic of the exemplary leaders at Miami-Dade, it does not profess to give a full description of the characteristic leadership style of any one of the administrators observed. Rather, it presents a composite view of the values, attitudes, and attributes that emerged as striking patterns occurring in the group as a whole.

Situational Leadership

SENSE OF DIRECTION

1. Thinks of future possibilities
2. Recognizes present momentum
3. Applies educational convictions
4. Thinks globally

STRUCTURE FOR IMPLEMENTATION

5. Respects expertise of others
6. Has a bias for action yet is flexible
7. Uses authority appropriately
8. Implements by increments

SENSE OF PERSONAL COMMITMENT

9. Acts positively
10. Acts with energy
11. Possesses motivational orientation
12. Possesses personal convictions

■FIGURE 14

Results of the analysis of the leadership at Miami-Dade produced a three-part model: (1) sense of direction or task orientation, (2) structure for implementation, and (3) sense of personal commitment and people orientation. These three major categories summarize the attributes observed among the leaders which have contributed, to a large degree, to the positive, achievement-oriented climate and the programs which are successfully meeting student needs at Miami-Dade. Without strong leadership, it is difficult to imagine the realization of the educational reforms which have taken place over the past decade and which have accounted for marked improvement in student achievement and satisfaction.

Furthermore, our study offers evidence and support for nearly every conclusion and recommendation set forth by the National Institute of Education (NIE) report, *Involvement in Learning* (1984). The "conditions of excellence" presented in the NIE report mirror the conditions which have been fostered by the leadership at Miami-Dade: (1) student involvement, (2) high expectations, and (3) assessment and feedback.

Although we feel that Miami-Dade has addressed nearly all the recommendations offered by the NIE report, the following have received particular emphasis from the leadership at the college over the past ten years and continue to guide decisions regarding the planning and implementation of new projects.

INCREASING STUDENT INVOLVEMENT

All colleges should offer a systematic program of guidance and advisement that involves students from matriculation through graduation. Student affairs personnel, peer counselors, faculty, and administrators should *all* participate in this system on a continuing basis (NIE, p. 31).

The Miami-Dade Student Flow System described earlier in this volume, resulting from years of collaboration among all levels of personnel, accomplishes the complex task of providing systematic guidance and advisement to all students from matriculation through graduation. The System entails a series of phases which warn students whose progress is unsatisfactory. This early warning system progressively increases intervention mechanisms for helping faltering students. If a student, after a number of warnings and interventions, fails to show satisfactory progress, he or she is placed on probation, which will eventually lead to dismissal if all attempts to assist the student in achieving satisfactory progress fail.

REALIZING HIGH EXPECTATIONS

> Faculties and chief academic officers in each institution should agree upon and disseminate a statement of the knowledge, capacities, and skills that students must develop prior to graduation (NIE, p. 39).

The administrative initiation and subsequent implementation of reading and writing components in all courses at Miami-Dade are manifestations of this recommendation. In addition, development of specific exit competencies in the five General Education core courses is further evidence of enactment of this recommendation at the college.

> Liberal education requirements should be expanded and reinvigorated to ensure that (1) curricular content is directly addressed not only to subject matter but also to the development of capacities of analysis, problem solving, communication, and synthesis, and (2) students and faculty integrate knowledge from various disciplines (NIE, p. 43).

Insistence by the administration and subsequent agreement among the faculty that five specifically developed, integrated General Education courses be a requirement, as well as twenty-three additional general education hours for every graduate, speaks to the need to prepare curricular content addressed to skill development as well as to subject matter acquisition. The initiation of the general-education required curriculum has necessitated the integration of knowledge from various disciplines as well as collaboration and team-teaching among faculty at Miami-Dade. The addition of reading and writing components to every course in the curriculum offered for credit is further evidence of the college's commitment to teaching students how to learn and to teaching skills necessary for living productively in society.

> Each institution should examine and adjust the content and delivery of the curriculum to match the knowledge, capacities, and skills it expects students to develop (NIE, p. 45).

The entire reform movement at Miami-Dade, which involved major changes and revisions in curriculum, was based on the competencies students need in order to become productive and to function effectively in an information-based society. Furthermore, the curriculum was adjusted to accommodate individual student needs by offering developmental courses at varying levels, depending on the skills of entering students.

> Community colleges, colleges, and universities should supplement the credit system with proficiency assessments both in liberal education and in the student's major as a condition of awarding degrees (NIE, p. 46).

The definition of specific exit criteria from courses in the curriculum at Miami-Dade is one answer to this recommendation.

> Institutions should offer remedial courses and programs when necessary but should set standards and employ instructional techniques in those programs that will enable students to perform well subsequently in college-level courses (NIE, p. 48).

"Access with excellence" is not an empty phrase at Miami-Dade, as evidenced in the practice of offering remedial courses at a number of levels. As the data have shown, at least 30% of the students beginning with remedial courses at the college have fared as well as or better than their university counterparts on the state-wide academic skills assessment exam.

> College presidents should strive to ensure that the behavior of their institutions evidences the ideals of honesty, justice, freedom, equality, generosity, and respect for others—the necessary values of community (NIE, p. 52).

The ability to confront unacceptable behavior and to relate decisions to a personal respect for all humankind are two outstanding qualities demonstrated by the administrators we observed at Miami-Dade. Without a doubt, these leaders expect ethical behavior and practice it themselves, thus creating a climate of high ethical standards which permeates the institution.

ASSESSMENT AND PROVIDING FEEDBACK

> Faculty and academic deans should design and implement a systematic program to assess the knowledge, capacities, and skills developed in students by academic and co-curricular programs (NIE, p. 55).

At Miami-Dade, the establishment through collaborative effort between faculty and administration of early warnings for students in trouble and congratulatory letters for those experiencing success requires systematic assessment of the knowledge, capacities, and skills developed in students. Furthermore, the use of specific exit criteria for courses is another example of Miami-Dade's response to this recommendation.

College officials directly responsible for faculty personnel decisions should increase the weight given to teaching in the processes of hiring and determining retention, tenure, promotion, and compensation, and should improve means of assessing teaching effectiveness (NIE, p. 59).

Every faculty member at Miami-Dade is evaluated every year. This policy is indicative of the college's commitment to teaching excellence. The administrators we interviewed emphasized the importance of formative rather than summative evaluation. That is, evaluation is a developmental process aimed at improving the quality of instruction and developing people. The development of a fair and effective faculty evaluation process is ongoing at Miami-Dade. Administrators expressed over and over the need to find the best process possible. In addition, release time, not an inexpensive commitment by the institution's leadership, was granted to faculty members for the purpose of preparing the five new General Education courses initiated by the reform.

The leadership competency model represented in the code book which was developed and used for examining the behaviors of Miami-Dade administrators was, to a very large extent, validated when the responses of subjects were analyzed using the Behavior Event Interviewing Technique (BEIT). That is, we found substantial evidence that the attributes outlined in the model were abundantly present among the excellent leaders we studied (see Figure 14 for model). Since the qualities represented in the model were derived from leadership theory espoused since the '60s (Dodds, 1962; Evans, 1970; Cohen & March, 1974; Kamm, 1982), as well as from a derivative sample of the data, the behaviors demonstrated by these administrators appear to reflect behavioral qualities which are linked with effective leadership. Therefore, in the following sections, we describe and illustrate the behavioral attributes which characterize the leadership responsible for initiating and implementing procedures and policies at Miami-Dade which account for improvements in morale among faculty and staff and in student achievement and satisfaction. Because most of these attributes were cited as critical to effective educational leadership by the NIE report and in previous research studies, we believe the competencies and the accompanying examples presented throughout the discussion provide general guidelines for improving administrative performance in the community college arena as well as in other higher educational settings.

SENSE OF DIRECTION

The leaders observed at Miami-Dade demonstrated a clear sense of direction. By this, we mean they (1) think of future possibilities, (2) recognize present momentum, (3) have and apply educational convictions, and (4) think globally.

Think of Future Possibilities

As Thomas Sergiovanni (1984) and others have noted, excellent leaders in educational institutions are not merely competent. Rather, they have a vision of what the college ought to be and work to instill an identifiable culture among the inhabitants of the organization. In other words, outstanding administrators are symbolic, cultural leaders who build an organizational climate and culture through selective attention to specific goals and behaviors. Their very actions clarify direction and build commitment leading to consensus regarding the organization's basic purposes. In response to our questions, Dr. Robert McCabe, President of Miami-Dade, conveys a sense of direction as well as insight into the demands of the future:

> My first place to look is the future. . . . If I designed an educational program for today, it would not be any good. You have to design educational programs for what the surrounding community is going to be in the future—five, ten years from now.

President McCabe undoubtedly sets the tone at Miami-Dade with his unwavering commitment and strong emphasis on the basic philosophy that equal access must be accompanied by a demand for high standards. This conviction, which he publicly states grows deeper all the time, helps to shape the entire institution. The administrators we interviewed expressed repeatedly in various ways the same values and concerns conveyed to us by the president. Most of the administrators we questioned had been at the college for over ten years, thus creating stability and continuity within the institution. Having shared values, these leaders, including the president, clearly demonstrate behaviors indicating a future orientation. That is, they (1) have vision, (2) relate decisions to a sense of institutional direction, (3) relate decisions to realistic possibilities for the college, (4) see important and necessary evidence to plot progress for the college, (5) use the institution's power and energy in planning and plotting progress for the college, and (6) promote future thinking in others. Thomas M. McKitterick, Dean of

Academic Affairs at Miami-Dade's South Campus, expresses an exuberance shared by the key leaders at the college: "I feel we have the ability to choose among unlimited opportunities. We can do what we wish to do and chart our own future."

In the same vein, the vice president who directs the North Campus, Terry Kelly, focuses clearly on where Miami-Dade is going in the following excerpt from his responses to our questions:

> High tech industry, the electronics age, is forcing the college to work more closely with the business and industry community, to be involved in more emphasis on retraining than entry level training to some extent, and to continue to stay in the "high tech" mode. Those are the major factors which are shaping the different directions the college is taking. College officials who are not in tune with the revolution, the electronic revolution, are going to be lost. And if they are not dealing with the ability of American industry, or the inability of American industry in many ways, to fully accommodate the tremendous retraining needs of the American work force, it is a mistake. That training is real. It's needed in so many ways, and community colleges will have a great future in dealing with that issue.

Along a different line of thinking, Jeffrey Lukenbill, Dean of Academic Affairs, North Campus, makes the observation,

> The concept of lifelong learning has taken hold with amazing speed—adults value continued learning more than ever was imagined fifteen years ago. The opportunity and challenge to meet adult needs and expectations call for dynamic responses which are not impeded by the state of the College bureaucracies.

These reactions are indicative of the first major competency in our leadership model: think of future possibilities. Vision and concern about the future of the college, tinged with a sense of urgency, influence the manner in which administrators make their day-to-day decisions.

Recognize Present Momentum

Outstanding leaders accent and draw upon the strengths of the college in order to promote constant improvement. Specifically, they recognize the present momentum at the college by (1) relating decisions to the historical strengths of the college (to the convictions of those who populate the institution), (2) relating decisions to a realistic assessment of current circumstances (educational, fiscal, and geographic), (3) relating decisions to a sense of where the college has been, (4) identifying forces from the environment that are helpful in moving the institution forward, and (3) fostering credibility through a coherent perspective leading to consistency and, therefore, to integrity.

Dean McKitterick demonstrates that he relates decisions to a realistic assessment of current circumstances while at the same time maintaining a future perspective:

> I know that the college is on a sound fiscal base and has excellent administration of fiscal matters; therefore, I feel anything is possible. In addition, the leadership of the college has continued to think five years ahead which is extremely important. Such leaders should not get bogged down in operations. I believe that an educational leader must be visionary and not too tied to a pragmatic present. I may be most useful when I am not busy with daily affairs. I am certain that this is true with the top leaders.

A final example indicative of the leadership competency "recognize present momentum" is given by the Dean of Nursing Education at the Medical Center Campus, Jeanne Stark. Her response shows that she identifies forces within the environment which are helpful in advancing the institution:

> I am very future oriented and feel that decisions made today must allow and prepare for those that I envision as inevitable. Nothing is static—a dynamic approach to education is vital. However, a sound informational base must be used. By that I mean what is happening in society, in education, in government that will influence the future. It is my job to be current and to share my information with my management team, and faculty and students when appropriate.

Apply Educational Convictions

Beginning with the president of a college, educational leadership, in order to be effective, must convey a strong commitment to learning and instruction. The leaders in a college, including the president, cannot simply practice sound principles of management and expect to achieve educational excellence. In order to lead a college effectively, administrators must demonstrate concern for instructional quality through their actions and values and the policies they set. There is no question the leaders at Miami-Dade exhibit a powerful commitment to learning and instruction. That is, they (1) have a well-formulated educational philosophy, (2) have a clear sense of priorities, (3) actively translate the college mission into student learning, (4) influence faculty behavior toward student learning, (5) consistently work to maintain and improve the institution's educational standards, and (6) are not afraid to use and exercise informed judgment.

Dean Stark offers a list of principles which influence her decisions regarding student learning. The list clearly represents a philosophy about learning held generally among the subjects of our study:

1. Students must be active participants in the process.
2. Students must be assisted to understand how they think and how that process affects behaviors.
3. Students must understand how the parts fit into the whole.
4. Students must clearly understand expectations and support systems.
5. There must be a recognition that all students are not equal— some need more help or time.
6. Experiential learning supports theoretical learning.
7. Students learn that which is made meaningful.
8. The teacher must be observant and caring as well as knowledgeable.
9. Students have the right to try to meet realistic goals within predetermined parameters but must be assisted to recognize strengths and limitations.
10. Faculty must be provided with the tools and setting that will assist them to facilitate the learning process.
11. Evaluation based on real data must help guide decisions related to change.

The conviction that all students can learn prevails among these educational leaders:

All students can learn and succeed providing they know what is expected of them and that race and economic or social background are not factors in learning (George Hedgespeth, Dean for Administration, Medical Center Campus).

A. All students can learn, regardless of their preparation, if they believe they can learn, if they have clear, stimulating teaching, and if they have adequate academic support.

B. Students have different, individual learning styles—the academic programs and classroom instruction must attempt to provide different learning and assessment opportunities.

C. Students learn at different rates—the challenge to develop systems that are not traditionally time bound is enormous.

D. Most students learn best through some experiential mode. More programs and courses should include interactive learning strategies.

The college mission has been truly translated into student learning when that learning is the focus and true referent point of all College activity.... I attempt to influence faculty behavior toward student learning by emphasizing on every available occasion that student learning is what we are all about. Policies and procedures, programs and courses should all be evaluated in terms of their contribution to student learning (Dean Lukenbill, Academic Affairs, North Campus).

Think Globally

A final competency under the major category "sense of direction" demonstrated by leaders at Miami-Dade is the ability to think globally. This critical attribute is indicated by the following behaviors: (1) thinking big (long term, higher principles, broader categories), (2) thinking and acting creatively, (3) seeing and conveying patterns of decision, (4) thinking ecologically or in terms of relationships, and (5) engaging in effective risk-taking in decisions affecting the future of the college, i.e., being innovative.

Global thinking has been found to increase in strength with administrative position level (Mullin, 1985). Because top administrators typically engage in more strategic types of activities than do middle-level positions, this phenomenon is somewhat predictable.

The horizon of the future varies from area to area. Staffing decisions have to be made in light of a future horizon which is one semester away. Training/retraining decisions must be made with an eye toward one or two years away. Special programming often must be viewed two or three years away. Demographics force longer-range futures to be considered, a decade or more is a useful horizon for this type of decision making. Each of these, and of course many others, must be taken into account. It is like a range of mountains that you view; each successive mountain, as they get further away from you, becomes a little less distinct and lighter in color. Each one is real and has substance, and you have to consider all of them to understand the range, but you have to tackle them one at a time—never forgetting that the entirety of the range is the ultimate problem (Vice President Jon Alexiou, Academic Affairs, District).

The community's disenchantment with educational institutions in general forces us to do some soul-searching. Technological possibilities force us to think differently about teaching/learning. Global concerns force us to think broadly about human aspirations and potentials (Kamala Anandam, Director, Computer-Based Instructional Development and Research).

One facet of this major competency area demands special attention and can best be described as innovation or risk-taking. It is clear from our investigation into the actions and behaviors of Miami-Dade administrators that they are willing to take risks.

We have good people and depth. We have been willing to take risks starting from the outset, with the board and with my predecessor. . . . By the way, you don't just decide you are going to take risks. You need a foundation of success to do it. When I go to the board, and I go to the board with things that sometimes they would disagree with or may have questions about whether we should be doing it or not, I go in with a base of always having given them good information—knowing what's going on, no surprises, a history of success. That's the base in which you can say, "Let's try this and see. We think it's a good idea, give us a chance to try it." So the willingness to take risks and the depth of people we can interest in continuing to learn from others about what's happening around us have been a foundation of a carefully nurtured reputation that we have in our community and out (President McCabe).

STRUCTURE FOR IMPLEMENTATION

A second major competency area demonstrated among the leaders at Miami-Dade, structure for implementation, is really an extension of the first major category, sense of direction. As discussed above, we found that these leaders provide a sense of direction through task-oriented behavior and by focusing on the basic purposes and direction of the college. These effective leaders also provide structure for implementing practices and policies in order to achieve the goals and purposes of the organization. They provide structure through a variety of means. First, they respect the expertise of others. Second, as Peters and Waterman (1982) have found, effective leaders possess a bias for action. Third, they use appropriate power and authority for an educational setting recognizing that a leader leads only with the consent of the governed. Finally, they implement by increments.

Respect Expertise in Others

Respect for others' expertise is manifested in the ways the leaders participating in our study interact with faculty, staff, and students. In general, we found that these leaders (1) show openly a respect for faculty, staff, and student expertise, (2) believe in the supremacy of the faculty in matters of its expertise on most educational matters, (3) know the limits of their own individual skill and authority, (4) are sensitive to the ideas, convictions, and feelings of others, (5) listen well, (6) handle well things initiated by others, (7) delegate responsibility clearly, effectively, and appropriately by matching individual strengths with the tasks, (8) grant autonomy when delegating assignments, having tolerance for mistakes, (9) have the ability to structure problems, meetings, and decisions so that responsibility may be allocated to associates, and, finally (10) communicate regularly with internal constituencies in a more or less formal manner.

Without a doubt, good leaders rely on good people. Dean McKitterick puts it this way: "The curriculum is what we are; the faculty provide the curriculum." Because of their respect for the talents and capabilities of others, effective administrators solicit input and listen well:

> I have twelve professionals reporting directly to me (associate deans and directors). Together they have over 150 years of experience at Miami-Dade. I have only three years, so I must listen a lot (Dean McKitterick).

> Faculty members must feel they are a part of the team. Their input is essential in developing an effective plan for student learning. Without their input and commitment, student learning will be negatively affected (Dean Kathleen Sigler, Administration, Wolfson Campus).

Blanca Gonzalez, Acting Associate Dean, Business Technical Division, North Campus, points out the necessity of freeing the faculty so that they can function effectively: "Faculty, inasmuch as possible, are isolated from the tedious day-to-day operations and 'paper shuffling' necessary to a unit the size of our division and of MDCC."

Finally, exceptional administrators know how to work effectively through others who have strengths in particular areas. They delegate responsibility effectively and grant autonomy realizing that mistakes will be made. That is, they allow room for the creative process to take place. Administrative support is thus an essential ingredient of cogent program planning and curricular operations. Vice President Kelly discusses this critical administrative behavior:

> When we start on a project, President McCabe stays behind us on everything. He doesn't waver a minute, and that's how we are able to get a great deal accomplished.... The philosophy is to get good people, give them good instruction, give them lots of room to move, lots of places to be creative, don't ride them, don't press them, trust them, and keep the project moving.

President McCabe also underscores the importance of decentralizing and working well through people:

> First, get people to come up with ideas about how to plan a project and how to implement it so that people are implementing their own thing. Secondly, never think you have all the answers. I don't know how many illustrations I can give of people having ideas that I thought had no chance at all to succeed. Earlier in my career I would have said I can't support that. Later on I came around to thinking people had a good case, and they were the kind of people whose judgment I respected, and they did the work to do it. Let them try. Maybe it will work. If you want a good system, you have to give people a chance to express themselves, especially with professional people. They must be given a chance to own, and do, and create throughout the institution.

Possess a Bias for Action

The leaders at Miami-Dade are shakers and movers, possessing a bias for action. Besides having a concern for good timing and a tendency to decide promptly unless there are reasons to delay, they exercise contingent leadership behavior. That is, these leaders alter methods and assign weights to concerns after assessing a particular situation. Having done so, they are flexible in their approach and choose courses of action appropriate to the situation. Furthermore, they are effective at collecting and integrating information. They take note of and analyze the context of decisions in order to understand the far-reaching ramifications of a deliberated action before settling on a specific direction. Perhaps most important, they solicit input from others in nearly all decision making.

Because good leaders depend heavily on the contributions of others, they are willing to change direction if new information requires them to do so. They do what the situation demands. The following excerpts illustrate how important they regard the opinions of others to be and how they go about obtaining consensus among staff:

> I attempt to get a wide range of points of view and information from a number of people in three categories: (1) experts on the issue, (2) recipients of the decision, and (3) administrators responsible for carrying out the decision. I attempt to give everyone an opportunity to participate. I keep adding elements until a consensus is reached (Vice President William Stokes, South Campus).

> When making a decision, I check data sources, check precedents in similar situations, consult with people who (either or both) (a) have an interest in the problem, (b) have knowledge, experience, and/or wisdom to bring to bear on the problem. At some point I have to decide that I have *enough* input and data to make the decision. I try to avoid the extremes of either (a) making the decision with no input or insufficient data (unless time *forces* this), or (b) waiting until I have all of the input (you never will or it will be too late anyway!) (Dean Daniel Derrico, Administration, North Campus).

Outstanding administrators show great concern about timely decisions. They act promptly unless there is good reason for delay. Making decisions under pressure often forces them to act *immediately*:

> You often must make a decision now, or very soon, without the luxury of enough time for all of the input, data collection, and analysis, consultation, etc. that you would like to have. In these cases you do the best you can, make the decision that seems best with what you have to work with, and move on.

You can usually make another decision later to minimize the damage if you are wrong. If not, you live with it, don't dwell on it, don't become defensive about it. Move on to the next problem! (Dean Derrico, North Campus).

The "bias for action" competency also includes the ability to think through the implications before making a decision. Vice President Lundgren of Medical Center Campus says she "visualizes the *impact* of alternatives—both immediate and long range" before taking a particular course of action.

In our study and generally throughout the leadership literature, we found that exceptional administrators demonstrate a great deal of flexibility in their day-to-day actions and decisions:

> I attempt to plan ahead by about a year through the formulation of appropriate goals. However, a strength I see myself as having is that of "shifting gears" midstream in order to adjust to the demands of a present, unplanned, but valuable project. One must possess the ability to continually readjust to be successful at Miami-Dade (and probably anywhere) (Dean Coppolechia, Wolfson Campus).

> My course of action really depends upon the scope of the goal. Often, if there is a realistic goal to achieve, the quicker one gets there, the better. On the other hand, if there's a long-term plan to stabilize enrollment, to build new programs, or to make some major shifts in the emphasis of the instructional program, a course of action is sometimes to try to move deliberately, touching all the bases and proceeding slowly so that when you finally get there you'll have built a foundation that won't crumble. . . . Again depending on the situations, there are several strategies that I have employed. Often it's out-and-out confrontation and head-on debate and let the chips fall where they may. Other times it's working on strategies to get supporters of those who disagree, personal friends of those who disagree or who are causing conflicts or problems, to get in the middle of the thing and help explain and support the administration's position. Often it's using outside people who give more credibility and more visibility to decisions so people can see them in another light. Often it's simply to ignore the criticism and move on and hope that in time it will pass (Vice President Kelly, North Campus).

One component of flexible behavior is the ability to maintain control over what one does with the time allotted. Hence, we asked these administrators how they keep their extremely busy schedules under control and what they do when they find themselves simply overextended. Their responses contain useful suggestions for administrators as well as others who hold pressure positions:

> Becoming overextended is a constant concern. There is no end of things that should be done. There is a constant need to prioritize. I actually review tasks periodically and ask: What is most important at this time? What can wait? What should I not try to do at all—because (1) I can't do it right anyway, or (2) it isn't worth the effort relative to other uses of my time and energy, or (3) it can be delegated to someone else who can do it just as well, and probably sooner. As to what to do about it, I sometimes go to my boss and say "time out! Let's see which of these things can be put on hold and also—no more special assignments or committees for a while!" (Dean Derrico, North Campus).

> Maintaining control of your life is one of the major problems. I get a stack of mail about ten inches high every day. I look at all my mail. I sort, pick out what I want to read, what I want to do, and what gets sent to someone else, etc. You can easily let what's in there describe your activity. It all is directing you, asking you to do something, wanting you to respond in some way—putting some restraint on you. The tough thing to do when that pile gets bigger is to step back from it and deal with it while keeping your own agenda and continuing to work (President McCabe).

Use Appropriate Power and Authority

We discovered that effective leaders at the college, while they recognize that there are many similarities between educational endeavors and businesses, also understand that the culture of a college campus differs in several major ways from the culture of a business or industrial firm:

> There is a relationship between the management of a college and that of a business in the process of identifying institutional goals and objectives, in providing incentives for achieving these

130

goals and objectives, in promoting group efforts and group solutions to problems, and in adopting positive personnel practices. There is a fundamental difference between the management of a business and of a college, in that the goal of a college is of a higher order of value—the realization of the potential of each student as contrasted to the achievement of profit for the business. The management of a college involves the enhancement of the individual—first the student, and then the faculty member—while the management of a business in the last analysis is impersonal since the good of the business subsumes the good of the individual workers (Dean Lukenbill, North Campus).

The subjects we observed are extremely canny in their assessment of the power structure of the college and the power inherent in their own positions. Describing the intrinsic power of their positions, these leaders show tremendous insight into the differences between power and influence:

> There is very little real power. There is responsibility but little real power. The power comes in the form of influence. I can influence faculty through suggestion and example, and I can influence the administration through well-reasoned and well-argued positions (Vice President Alexiou, District).

> The power in my position is not so much the authority to command and direct, but more the opportunity to motivate and inspire. The greatest exercise of my power is to work with the administrators and faculty who report to me to identify goals, to plan, and to execute with dedication and integrity. I have a tremendous opportunity to exercise my power to bring individuals together to pursue common goals and not to tolerate incompetence and inefficiency. Attempts to exercise my power by threats or by apparent superiority would be a mockery of authority and a deterrent to achievement of goals (Dean Lukenbill, North Campus).

These leaders understand and recognize the decentralized authority structure of a college, they understand the informal power structure, and they are effective in resolving conflict. An outstanding feature of their actions is a willingness to confront what could be potentially destructive situations:

I deal with conflict directly; I try to get the parties together; I try to find out what has caused the conflict. I research any college policies related to the conflict, talk with the other people when necessary. Many times the conflicts I encounter need to be dealt with appropriately at another level. I try to follow through and see that the chair or faculty members have solved the problem (Margaret Pelton, Associate Dean, Humanities, South Campus).

When my course of action is challenged, I first ask why. If there is a good reason, I can hear it and look for an alternate approach. If the challenge is invalid, I attempt to change the challenger's mind through explanation of my reasoning. Sometimes the discussions become heated and loud, but I do not feel that is necessarily unhealthy. Sometimes I use a third person to assure listening is taking place on both sides (Dean Stark, Medical Center Campus).

Finally, it is interesting to note that this competency, "appropriate use of power and authority within an educational setting," appeared to be the most powerful predictor of position level of the twelve competencies assessed among this sample of administrators (Mullin, 1985).

Implement by Increments

The final competency area under the major category "structure for implementation" demonstrated by administrators at Miami-Dade is the practice of getting things done step by step and little by little. These leaders readily bounce back from temporary setbacks and appreciate that slow change is progress. Furthermore, they relish partial successes. An important component of this competency area is the ability to live comfortably with ambiguity. These leaders accomplish success by avoiding ultimatums. They never become dogmatically wed to their way of doing things. On the contrary, they encourage and praise alternative and even contradictory approaches. Whenever their course of action is challenged, they are effective in the resolution of the dissonance.

The following examples show more specifically how the leaders at Miami-Dade move the institution forward by breaking tasks into achievable steps, and how they motivate faculty and staff to accomplish as many of the steps as possible:

In the past I favored rapid movement only to find myself sweeping up hurt feelings by the wayside and asking myself, "So now
this goal has been attained; so what?" The fun in life is possessing a goal and proceeding through the motions for its attainment. After one goal is achieved, the healthy individual seeks
another. The key is to savor the ritual of the steps toward attainment. The attainment is often anticlimactic. However, if
the progress is too slow one is bogged down in frustration. The
worst state of all, of course, is having no goal; i.e., depression
(Jane MacDonald, Associate Dean, South Campus).

I favor subdividing a long-range goal into smaller manageable
objectives. I like to move quickly in achieving an objective
which causes me to move closer to achieving a goal in a
reasonable amount of time.... I am but a part of the college
community, and, therefore, there are bound to be differences
between my desire and what I am able to accomplish. With
long-range goals and emphasis on the process, these differences
do not seem to bother me much (Dean Schinoff, South
Campus).

SENSE OF PERSONAL COMMITMENT

The third and final major category of the leadership competency
model which has emerged from our analysis of the behaviors, attitudes,
and values of administrators at Miami-Dade is a sense of personal commitment to the job and to people. Although all three competency areas
are essential for achieving a high quality of leadership, a strong personal commitment may well be the most basic of all three areas. In
Mullin's (1985) analysis of administrator responses, she found that a
sense of powerful commitment was the most prevalently demonstrated
quality among the Miami-Dade leaders interviewed. This finding suggests that exemplary leadership must begin with this behavioral component, for it is difficult to imagine successful demonstration of the
other behavioral competencies represented in our leadership model
without it.

Four attributes lend substance to the everyday practices required for
administering the business of an exemplary college: (1) having a positive
outlook, (2) possessing personal energy, (3) having the ability to motivate
others through employing good interpersonal skills, (4) possessing personal convictions and integrity.

Positive Action

A striking quality exhibited by the leaders we studied at Miami-Dade is a clear sense of self and a great deal of self-respect in facing day-to-day problems. A second compelling quality is the tendency to discern the best in everyone in every circumstance. Third is the ability to admit mistakes and tolerate self-failures. A fourth characteristic related to a sense of personal commitment is the tendency to redirect thinking from seeing issues as problems to viewing them as challenges. Fifth, leaders rarely take things personally but rather see themselves as part of the system, a characteristic which harkens back to global thinking. Finally, and perhaps most important of all the specific attributes discussed so far, they love their work but maintain a healthy balance between their careers and their personal lives:

> I love coming to work every day. I also love my weekends and vacations because it does wear on you after a while. But I do not see my job as "problems." I see it as the very normal process of getting things done within the limited time, energy, and resources that we can bring to bear. That is a challenge. . . One thing I heard years ago, I have always believed and remembered. I cannot recall who said it, but it is: "You should always take your responsibilities very seriously, but you should never take yourself too seriously" (Dean Derrico, North Campus).

> There's never any day that's the same. It is exciting to be on a college campus. I come with enthusiasm; sometimes the harder the problems, the more interesting it is to work on them. The challenging aspect of the job is that every day is going to be different; there's going to be some tough problems that make you stand tall. There's going to be satisfying moments and lots of frustrations, but it is a fun job making major contributions to learning, providing opportunities to students for moving in new directions, and bringing a lot of satisfaction to large numbers of people if our learning programs are doing what they are supposed to be doing (Vice President Kelly, North Campus).

Optimism abounds throughout the responses given by these key leaders at Miami-Dade. They are realistic as well as positive in their approach to the daily challenges an administrator encounters:

> My "desires" are, at this point, less rigid and allow for "surprise" outcomes from time to time. I am comfortable with what

I am able to accomplish (Vice President Lundgren, Medical Center Campus).

No problem is worth getting an ulcer over! Back up, relax, take a deep breath, keep the problems in perspective, and then do the best possible job you can with the energy and resources you possess (James Harvey, Associate Dean, South Campus).

Blanca Gonzalez explains how she attempts to redirect thinking from problems into productive situations:

I am a firm believer in negotiation rather than confrontation. I also try to avoid "no-win" situations. I try to determine who the challengers are and what the challenges are. I try to follow this by honest, open discussion. I have always felt that professional disagreements are healthy and conducive to improvement.

Another technique for viewing problems in a more positive light used by these administrators is recognizing the assets of the people with whom they work:

I try to be aware of all of the positive and negative strengths of all of the people I work with. I find that the more I involve my staff in different activities, the more I learn about their abilities. I like very much to teach people about areas they know little about, and involve them in problem-solving activities that are new to them. All of this provides me with a continued fresh look at the most routine matters, as well as new solutions I wouldn't have thought of (Dean Sigler, Wolfson Campus).

I think one of my strengths is that I do recognize assets held by other people because you really can't be an effective leader if you don't. Lots of skills and talents need to come to bear on having a good institution and the best way to build self-respect in others is to give them that free range, give them that support and the reward structure of the visibility, the exposure, the acknowledgments when good work is being done in placing them in the right positions where they can be recognized for good work so they can feel good about themselves (Vice President Kelly, North Campus).

135

Personal Energy

We found that the exemplary leaders at the college set an example of dedication and enthusiasm by generating the required energy for meeting difficult challenges. They frequently work alongside the people they direct, demonstrating their commitment to a course of action.

Furthermore, these leaders initiate rather than respond. Dedication and persistence have been cited by authors who write about organizational behavior as qualities which result in professional success and effectiveness. The following excerpts reveal the kind of tenacity and persistence which lead to professional efficacy:

> We wanted to close off a street that runs through the campus to traffic, but the local merchants were all opposing it, so we weren't successful. But I found a way to offer to the merchants another street that could be made two-way instead of remaining one-way, if they would allow us to shut down one block of this other street. They agreed if I could convince the transportation people. It all worked out and we now have a broad avenue on campus for outdoor events (Dean Sigler, Wolfson Campus).

> I like challenges. My energy level rises when someone says "No" to an idea that my staff and I think is fantastic and should be supported. The more complex the project the more energy I can muster to be involved. As an example, I instituted a Quality Circle Program that many said I could not do. After two years, it has just about been phased out, but it served its purpose (Dean Schinoff, South Campus).

Finally, they remember to manage unobtrusively. Wayne Silver, Associate Dean of Communication at North Campus, illustrates the example these leaders set for others:

> I think I'm one of the luckiest people alive to be able to work at something that I enjoy and that I think is important. I think I'm twice blessed because I work with people I love and respect, people who share similar commitments. That's heartfelt and it's genuine, and I think it shows. I have an excitement for what I do and a real belief in what I do and I cherish the people with whom I work. I appeal to personal pride. I do that consciously and unconsciously, I guess. Because I believe in the basic nobility of this place and in the nobility of what we

do, I tend to appeal to that in people. If I have a strength, it's that.

Motivational Orientation

While the leaders we studied at Miami-Dade have high expectations of themselves and others, they are extremely supportive of people and possess warm interpersonal skills. In this way, they are successful at motivating others while nurturing self-respect. Dean John Losak explains how he helps those he directs to grow and improve: "I attempt to build self-respect in people by precisely and intentionally reinforcing their assets and by never criticizing their personhood—only, and then rarely, their work." President McCabe adds, "Most important is to let people know you trust them. The most important way to show you trust them is to give responsibility and don't second guess."

Exemplary leaders use humor effectively and demonstrate empathy for those with whom they work. Dean Stark comments, "Without a sense of humor you'd better not try to deal with others at all." Blanca Gonzalez states, "Like the comic relief in a Greek tragedy, life is too serious not to have some room for humor." Vice President Alexiou emphasizes the significant part humor plays in his interactions with others:

> Humor is absolutely indispensable in dealing with others. Humor can take the bite out of decisions, and it can help create a shared environment. Without humor, two-hour meetings would seem like six (and not just four).

And finally,

> Humor is an individualized personality trait that can work well for you if you are comfortable with it. It can ease tensions, facilitate team building, and add to an element or environment that this is a fun place to work. In all modesty I would think that if I was rating my own strengths I would consider that to be one. Humor is a very important part of my everyday administrative style. This is a part of how I function day-to-day either inside or outside the institution. There can be some drawbacks if one's humor is inappropriate or one becomes flip at the wrong times, or tries to joke away serious matters. So humor has to be tempered with some good judgment and good balance, but it certainly has a place, and, in my assessment, it is a very important administrative skill applied at the right time, with the right level of intensity (Vice President Kelly).

137

Along with humor, prevalent among the leaders we studied was genuine empathy for others, especially in situations requiring difficult decisions. Margaret Pelton of South Campus offers this comment: "One of the hardest things for people to do is to cause pain in another person. I try to face tough decisions and strategize how the pain can be as little as possible." Dean Lukenbill adds,

> Empathy is not sympathy that supports another's inappropriate dependency or avoidance. I try to listen carefully and critically. I try to demonstrate that I listen by using suggestions, supporting efforts, and responding with concrete behaviors.

These responses reveal that the leaders we observed regard people as more important than procedures. They listen, communicate, and develop a good rapport with the people they direct. They are approachable and work constantly to keep all communication channels open and unclogged by trivia.

> My office door is open at all times. If it is closed it means you should not walk into the office. If it's open, even if someone is in there, you can come in. You don't have to knock. . . . The only time I really close my door is on personnel situations, because that is very privileged, a confidential exchange between myself and a staff member (James Harvey).

One mechanism these leaders use for improving communication is to give early signals in order to avoid confrontation; management-by-walking-around is another. Finally, they work hard to create coherence among staff, encouraging them to work together as a team. Dean Derrico of North Campus gives a good illustration of how coherence is created and the focus on trivialities is reduced:

> I do not waste a lot of energy playing games, telling and keeping track of different stories, minding everybody else's business, or hating any person or group. These things are energy-sapping and self-destructive. I think positive. I think things can be done. I love my job. I believe in my work, my profession, my college.

Personal Convictions

Miami-Dade's exemplary leaders value people above everything else. As Vice President Lundgren puts it, "People are the product in our area of responsibility. Products such as written materials are just 'tools.'" The leaders reveal a general respect and high regard for all in their belief in people and in their strong commitment to the development of faculty and staff either through involvement or formal training. Recognizing that interpersonal relations are more essential to an administrator's success than are managerial skills, they emphasize the importance of people over product. Consider the following responses in this light:

> I emphasize the importance of people over product by not making unreasonable demands on people (I very rarely ask anyone to stay late to complete a task; I almost never call them at home), and by continually reminding myself that they have lives and interests beyond their work (Dean John Losak, Institutional Researcher, District).

> I try to work within a philosophy that I don't ask people to do a job that I haven't done and wouldn't do myself. Sometimes that means doing things outside of what you are directly responsible for (Dean George Hedgespeth, Medical Center Campus).

> I am enough of a humanist, beneath my business officer exterior, to believe that people are most important, that a single individual has value, rights, dignity, and commands respect. People should be treated with justice and compassion. This must not be sacrificed for any product because this is one of the core values—indeed the primary core value and moral principle—of our nation and of our college (Dean Derrico, North Campus).

Vice President Stokes, South Campus, offers these maxims:
1. Be truthful.
2. Be consistent.
3. Be relaxed and confident.
4. Use "we," not "I."
5. Remember where you came from. Good people need opportunities and challenges to succeed.

Outstanding leaders work hard to be fair and recognize that people have a right to know about issues which directly affect them: "I try to alert them in advance. I feel that people should not be taken by surprise," says Kamala Anandam, Director of Computer-Based Instructional Development and Research for the Miami-Dade District.

A belief in human potential is characteristic of these leaders; they give credit and recognition to others for their accomplishments. President McCabe's convictions about human potential are apparent in the following illustration:

I believe that nobody fully realizes his potential and that everybody has potential. It may be greater or smaller, but there is value in everyone. Part of our task is to try to get people—individuals—to realize and take advantage and feel good about themselves; to try to get students to understand what they can do, what values they have. Everyone is not going to be able to do the same thing. If the criterion for success were to be a ballet dancer, I would be in trouble. But I can probably learn to do something. There may be something else I can do well. There is potential in everyone that should be developed regardless at which level it turns out to be.

Others offer their views on human potential:

Human potential, given the proper motivation and leadership, can accomplish virtually any goal and overcome virtually any problem. That is not to say that each individual has the exact same amount of potential, or is capable of sustaining an equal amount of effort to achieve the goal. But everyone can move from where he is to some "better" state (Vice President Alexiou).

I believe human potential is limitless. Properly motivated and given adequate resources, a human being can accomplish practically anything (Dean Hedgespeth).

As for reward and recognition, Dean Sigler offers comments which represent the general attitude of the subjects of our study:

The most important aspect of [motivating and influencing others] is to provide positive recognition and reward for faculty when deserved. Such recognition does not always have to be a monetary reward—yet, that certainly helps! . . . Rewarding and recognizing positive behavior is a key to building self-respect. I think it is important the staff members know that not only do I know of the good work they do, but that my boss has been informed also.

While willing to confront and correct inappropriate behavior, they also demonstrate concern for people in tough decisions. However, despite difficult situations, they have integrity and remain true to their values.

In conclusion, through our analysis of the actions, values, and skills of key leaders at Miami-Dade, we believe that a model of leadership excellence worthy of emulation by others in the field of community college education has emerged. "I think that we are especially important because we are trying to demonstrate to the country that you can have open access and high quality in the same context," President McCabe says. This commitment is echoed throughout the institution by administrators, support staff, and faculty.

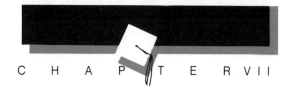

C H A P T E R VII

EXCELLENT TEACHERS

Wh

hat distinguishes a great teacher? Most of us can recall great teachers we've known, although we may not be able to explain precisely why they were "great." This is what researchers study: What makes these teachers different? What sets them apart? The literature on teaching effectiveness and the results of our study confirm that there is a core of characteristics which are central to excellent teaching. These characteristics, as exemplified by the excellent teachers we studied at Miami-Dade Community College, are the focus of this chapter.

College research on teaching effectiveness can be categorized as process-outcome, qualitative, or descriptive (Ellner & Barnes, 1983). Process-outcome studies examine the relationship between actions and the results incurred by those actions—in other words, how the kind of teaching affects what the students learn. Qualitative studies observe everything that is going on and attempt to piece together a process. They look at real situations with the assumption that understanding can be gained only by the participants; therefore, qualitative research includes a level of interaction that precedes the development of theories. Descriptive studies focus on gathering data about the teaching process, either through a rating system, such as a five-point scale; a sign system which marks whether a behavior is observed within a time frame or not; or a category system in which an event is recorded when it occurs (Ellner & Barnes, 1983). The category system is used in this research.

There are several ways to conceptualize occurrences. One is to select a characteristic, go into a classroom, and look for it. Another is to identify effective teachers and observe what those teachers do. We combined these techniques in our study. What we found was an overwhelming affirmation that, indeed, great teachers have certain definable characteristics, a combination of which makes up the "right stuff." Here we describe what that "stuff" is and in what ways it may be manifested. How those characteristics are combined and used may become the distinguishing factor between the excellent and the average.

We sent Miami-Dade teachers and administrators a list of the twelve Selection Research Institute (SRI) themes, which we feel reflect well the literature on characteristics of effective teachers. Teachers and administrators were asked to nominate two teachers they felt best exemplified these qualities. The number of nominations was tallied, and those candidates who received the most votes were selected from each campus. From over a thousand full-time instructors at the college, seventeen professors were thus chosen, in proportionate numbers from each campus, with the largest campus selecting six nominees and the smallest selecting three. There were numerous ties, which were broken by the college president. Our methodology required that we limit our sample to a relatively small group, so the following seventeen were selected to represent the faculty as a whole:

> Thelma Altshuler, Arts/Sciences, Mitchell Wolfson Campus
> Jack Bateman, Biology, South Campus
> Robert Blitzer, Mathematics, South Campus
> M. Paige Cubbison, History, South Campus
> Betty Ferguson, Language Institute, North Campus
> Jack Gill, Math/Physics, North Campus
> James Gray, Occupational Education, Mitchell Wolfson Campus
> Phyllis Greenfield, Nursing Education, Medical Center Campus
> Alice Huff, Arts/Sciences, Medical Center Campus
> Roslyn Reich, Secretarial Careers, North Campus
> Margaret Rose, English Core, South Campus
> Candido Sanchez, Natural Sciences, Mitchell Wolfson Campus
> Louise Skellings, Communication, North Campus
> Roberta Stokes, Physical Education, South Campus
> Tonie Toney, Physics/Earth Science, South Campus
> William Weaver, Arts/Sciences, Medical Center Campus
> Reina Welch, Arts/Sciences, Mitchell Wolfson Campus

The teachers who were rated as excellent by their supervisors and peers received an extensive questionnaire in which they were asked to describe in detail their teaching behaviors. We followed these questionnaires with personal interviews conducted on their home campuses using the Behavioral Events Interview Technique (BEIT). The BEIT is an operant assessment technique, developed by David McClelland (1978), which assumes that if individuals have a certain quality they will mention it even if the quality is not specifically named. This technique has had wide validation; we, too, found it to be most effective.

The responses to our questionnaires were coded against the twelve SRI teaching themes. At that time, a thirteenth theme that appeared consistently among our sample of excellent teachers was added to the original twelve. Using Klemp's categories for grouping the characteristics of superior performance from people in all career fields, the thirteen themes were divided into three divisions: motivation, interpersonal skills, and intellectual skills. These divisions served to organize the general teaching themes. (See Figure 15.)

MOTIVATION

According to Klemp, motivation is a key factor in the successful performance of any job. Motivation is defined by Klemp (1977) as "a need state—a prerequisite for behavior" (p. 107). We began our investigation by looking at the factors that appeared to motivate these teachers, the reasons they aspired to perform exceptionally well. As we looked for motivating factors, we also noted the interpersonal and intellectual themes that were present in the responses of these successful instructors.

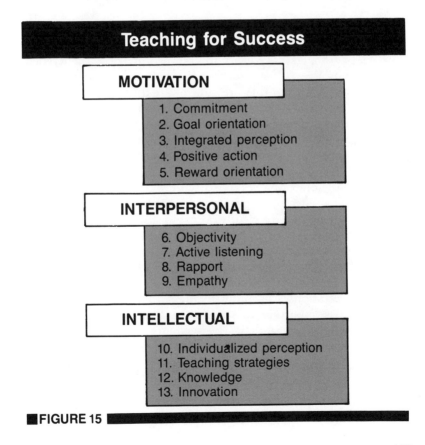

Teaching for Success

MOTIVATION
1. Commitment
2. Goal orientation
3. Integrated perception
4. Positive action
5. Reward orientation

INTERPERSONAL
6. Objectivity
7. Active listening
8. Rapport
9. Empathy

INTELLECTUAL
10. Individualized perception
11. Teaching strategies
12. Knowledge
13. Innovation

■FIGURE 15

Long-term Commitment

Excellent teachers have a heartfelt commitment to teaching. They enjoy sharing information and feel a strong sense of meaning in the teacher-student relationship. Cohen and Brawer (1977) found that community college teachers wish to spend more time, rather than less, in the classroom with students. Wilson, Gaff, Dienst, Wood, and Bavry (1975) found that effective teachers show a greater commitment to teaching and enjoy it more. Another study found that teachers who want to teach more are the ones chosen by students as superior (Miller, 1974). Most of the teachers who were selected for the study at Miami-Dade have been there for more than ten years and express the desire to stay until retirement. Professor James S. Gray's remarks are typical: "I expect to teach as long as I am competent to do so. I thoroughly enjoy teaching and have no ambitions beyond being a good classroom teacher."

High Expectations

Excellent teachers have every intention of making a difference in their students' lives. Of course, they mean to affect students through their subject matter, but they are quite aware that they hold the power to have a profound impact on the students assigned to them. This belief that they can teach assumes that students can learn, for a teacher can have no impact unless the learner also chooses to be influenced. Excellent teachers believe in their own efficacy (Farrar, Neufeld, & Milse, 1984).

Believing in someone's ability to achieve has been fondly dubbed "the Pygmalion effect." It appears to motivate profoundly some people's achievement and frequently occurs in student-professor relationships. The excellent instructors at Miami-Dade encourage student achievement by their expectations. Not only do these instructors expect great performance in academic areas, but they expect attitudes to measure up to their standards as well.

High expectations can produce pressure for insecure students; therefore, it is important to set those expectations in a supportive climate that will allow students the freedom to be creative, to try, fail, try again, and succeed:

> My students know that I expect them to produce their best for me, but I try to alleviate the pressure by assuring them that I won't get upset if they make a mistake, only if they won't try (Professor Betty Ferguson).

Sometimes the skills expected have not been taught or have not been learned previously. Effective teachers do not let this impede their progress; they accept the challenge and incorporate the new material.

Teachers also model the skills they want their students to know. Professor Thelma Altshuler illustrates: "I take notes on the board as a demonstration of what they should do as they watch televised lectures."

Meeting the high expectations of these professors requires hard work on the part of the students. But the students choose to do the work because it brings self-satisfaction. Their efforts pay off for them, and they feel proud of their work.

The literature on teaching often includes references to pitching instruction to a "steering group," a group of students used as "benchmarks" to determine comprehension, pacing and the need for further practice (Good, Biddle, & Brophy, 1975). At the college level, this practice is cited by Brown and Thornton (1963), who suggest that the optimum point be determined by the instructor's knowledge of the performance levels of the students. In general, the higher the ability and achievement of the steering group in a classroom, the higher the learning shown by the class as a whole. Teachers who aim higher generally produce better results (Billips & Rauth, 1984). These high expectations and resulting successes produce positive results for students, including higher self-esteem, a higher self-concept regarding ability, and an improved internal locus of control, all of which often transfer to areas outside the classroom (Medley, 1979). And since these attitudes correlate with success, they may also correlate with achievement, motivation, and behavior.

Excellent teachers develop good study and organizational habits in their students. According to both the research literature and findings in our study, teachers demonstrate their high expectations by modeling, by making demands on students, and by helping them set and achieve goals. They model such behaviors as punctuality, organization, emphasis on academic tasks, and neatness (Glassman, 1980). They demand attention in class, and care and accuracy in student work. Each of these small tasks helps a student feel his or her work is important; as each task is accomplished well, the student is made to feel successful.

The standards at Miami-Dade Community College are more rigorous than those of many other colleges, and they are more consistent across departments. Excellent teachers attest to the importance of maintaining high expectations and finding ways to move students along a continuum from entry level skills to proficiency.

Instill Student Responsibility

Effective teachers make students accountable for their learning. College teachers believe that students, because they have chosen to come, are in class to learn. Tyler (1958) observed that both student motivation and high standards of performance set by the learner were conditions for effective learning. This principle appears no less true today. Excellent teachers expect students to attend class, take notes, study, do assignments, ask questions in class, and make arrangements for extra help as necessary:

> If students have shortcomings which hinder their progress in my course, I expect them to take responsibility for improvement rather than waste time indulging in the "blame game" (Professor Toney).

> I expect students to accept their responsibilities and their roles as participants in the learning process. I help them understand that we must work together—but that it will take work (Professor Stokes).

In sum, these teachers make the students take full responsibility, all the while encouraging them to meet the challenge, and cheering enthusiastically when they succeed. They help students realize that success is not based on external factors like luck, but on their own ability to harness their talents, seize opportunities, and work arduously to understand their lessons. These teachers foster independence in their students by giving them the tools to learn for themselves.

Available for Extra Help

Schneider, Klemp, and Kastendiek (1981) found that effective instructors are accessible outside of class, and they are available to average as well as to superior students. Roueche (1982) found that effective teachers have a commitment to the profession. Wilson et al. (1975) found this quality to be the single greatest delineator between effective faculty and their colleagues. Their results showed that the amount of interaction outside of class multiplies the effect such teachers have on students. It seems reasonable to assume that a teacher who is available before and after class or during office hours is more likely to have good rapport with students, see them as individuals, and be perceived as enthusiastic. Garrison (1967) reported that community college instructors are student-centered, and Cohen and Brawer (1977) agreed.

We found that excellent faculty members are available not only for extra help in their classes, but also for college projects, student clubs, and the like. These instructors give of their time and expertise in many ways that support the actual classroom function. These teachers are fully committed to their profession and to their students. They value what they do and feel it is a very real contribution to society. They are actively involved in making the educational process succeed, and their zeal attests to it.

GOAL ORIENTATION

Every learning field yields a vast conglomeration of facts, constructs, theories, and principles. In order to make sense of the subject, teachers limit the parameters of their investigation by adopting goals. Specific goals help them narrow the field of the subject matter and provide a focus for instruction. A similar process is applied as they set goals in their own personal lives and again as they help students set goals.

Set Personal Goals

People who set personal goals and seek personal models for themselves are motivated to excel. In our study, the majority of participating teachers establish such goals and determine a course of action for attaining them. By clarifying their values into manageable goals, these exemplary teachers set up a clear path to follow in reaching their objectives:

> I pursue my goals by following the techniques of goal setting. I establish my objectives, identify steps to achieve them, try to anticipate obstacles I may face, and identify methods for measuring my success (Professor Stokes).

Family and spiritual values are often cited as inspirational motivation by the teachers we studied. Perhaps their strong commitment to these values provides a foundation for an understanding of their own role in inspiring and supporting their students:

> I establish direction in my life through a number of means: 1) by being conscious of certain priorities, such as my religious commitment, my family, and my commitment to my job; 2) by trying to assess accurately the areas where I have skills and talents, and the areas where I am not particularly skilled; 3) by trying to achieve some sort of balance in which I can grow

151

and develop personally and also be of some positive value to other people (Professor Rose).

These people know the value of positive thinking and keep their talents in mind as they assess ways to go about reaching their goals. They constantly think in terms of potential success and measure their steps toward it. This frame of mind is a trait typical of successful people and appears to correlate positively with high-achieving students. (It will be addressed in more detail in this chapter under *Positive Attitude*.)

Set Student Goals

Excellent teachers also set goals for their students and help them to reach these goals. They carefully detail course outlines which set out clearly what they want and how they want it. Brown and Thornton (1963) refer to an understanding of the goals as a prerequisite for learning. Then effective teachers help students move toward the achievement of these goals. They believe that a course of action can be followed to a successful end.

Moving students toward academic and personal goals is an important task to exceptional teachers, as is illustrated by the comments of Professor Gray:

> I believe that these students have goals and directions in their lives just as I have, and I am part of the process by which they will achieve these goals.

INTEGRATED PERCEPTION

Exceptional teachers have a holistic view of both their students and their subject matter. We refer to this characteristic as "integrated perception." Students are seen as whole individuals operating in a broader context beyond the classroom. This view of students influences an excellent teacher's approach to teaching, classroom examples, and methods used to illustrate concepts. Brown and Thornton (1963) suggest that this perspective can improve teaching. Miller (1972) finds this characteristic indicative of excellence.

Exceptional college teachers appear to possess an integrated perception more often than do high school teachers (Roueche, Baker, with Mullin & Omaha Boy, 1985). The large majority of college teachers in our study demonstrated the ability to perceive the "big picture." As one excellent instructor says,

> In addition to looking at my students as "students," I see them
> as whole persons with problems and strengths. I strive to be
> a teacher-facilitator; we all learn together (Professor Reich).

Most of these instructors have had more than ten years of experience
in teaching. It is possible that excellent teachers who have less experience may not demonstrate this quality; or it may be that adult
students are more aware of the need to relate themselves and their
coursework to the greater whole and therefore make more demands
on professors to provide the connections for them.

Creating an interactive perspective for subject matter is another way
effective teachers show their integrated perception. They do not see
their classrooms as isolated glimpses of the truth, but rather as a part
of the whole that lends authority to the truth:

> Never forgetting that the rest of academic disciplines are just
> as important as my own and convincing the students that this
> material has to be integrated with what they are learning in
> humanities, English, social studies, and science is my attitude.
> I relate current events in my field to other disciplines such as
> history, government, and the sciences. I stress the importance
> of reading and writing (Professor Gray).

Integrated perception among exceptional teachers provides unity and
continuity in daily lessons and further develops an understanding of
facts and concepts from a more macroscopic view. Holistic teaching
develops the total individual and helps students link the knowledge
gained in the classroom to life in the total environment. Through this
process, learning becomes meaningful, useful, and relevant for every
student.

Integrated perception is also a quality that sensitive people use to
create their world view. By seeing students outside the classroom and
by integrating subject matter into general learning, they share a perspective useful in their own self-perception:

> Actually I can't think of individual accomplishments as mean-
> ing as much as the evolution of my attitudes and insights over
> the years. I can now deal with students and situations more
> successfully than before (Professor William Weaver).

Such individuals internalize understanding for the purpose of more
useful service to others. This is a sophisticated quality and worthy of
further study.

POSITIVE ATTITUDE

The most powerful quality these teachers have is their understanding of how to use a positive orientation to help students achieve. They bring to their students a supportive attitude, a willingness to do whatever is necessary to help them succeed. And, of course, they believe in their own ability to succeed. Their attitudes transform their teaching, bringing it to a higher level, a more productive standard.

The link between teacher and learner is of prime consequence. Knowing that success can be programmed, knowing that the instructor is capable of success, and then transferring that knowledge to the student to enable continued success is a powerful tool:

> Visualization has tremendous potential in education. I visualize myself as a successful teacher; I visualize myself in important, new situations. I visualize myself in control. I conceive, believe, and achieve (Professor Reich).

Believe in the Power of Success

These excellent teachers are able to cut through the fear, the lack of confidence, and the lack of knowledge to share with their students a vision of achievement. They convey their concern in a positive manner that inspires the students with the desire to succeed. They do not assume that students will learn only if they want to learn; instead, these teachers see their job as being a motivating force to cause good performance. They believe in their students, and they believe in their teaching:

> I approach the academically deficient student as a challenge to my ability to teach the student something that will make a difference in his life. Most students who are difficult to motivate are so because of their fear of failure. If I can get them to face that fear, things seem to move forward (Professor Ferguson).

> I see students as mostly very young people who have the capacity for learning, like sponges in that respect, but sponges often with the outer pore spaces clogged with misconceptions about their potential, about science in general, and about college in general (Professor Toney).

The teachers manifest a powerfully positive attitude, which both challenges and inspires their students to achieve. This spirit incorporates their expectations, visions, and caring. They act with compassion, understanding, a spirit of adventure, and excitement.

154

Believe That Teacher Promotes Learning through Success

Great teachers know that expectation alone does not produce results in the classroom. Each seed that is planted is carefully watered and nurtured so that growth can occur. In a college setting, no less than any other learning environment, students are taught how to progress through the learning cycle.

The excellent teachers we studied believe that they are responsible for promoting learning through successes. They set up circumstances in which the students can experience success. Teachers know that they have influence in their classrooms, and they use their power constructively to aid learning:

> From the first day of class on, I stress the fact that I am there to help them, that the reason I teach is because I love to teach and that their success is my success (Professor Welch).

> Student success is the school's reason for existence (Professor Reich).

Reward Successful Behaviors

These teachers not only structure their teaching to plan for success, but when it comes, they reward the behaviors that they want to see. Everything, from notes of praise to hugs, is possible in the positive environments created by these caring, loving, and supportive teachers:

> I heap oral praises on my students daily. I also write little notes of praise on their assignments and exams for them to "show off" to their family and friends (Professor Ferguson).

> I read the names of students who earn A grades on exams and congratulate them individually in class. I also ask these students to describe briefly their personal study method that helped them to succeed.... When I find a question or observation to be interesting, well-structured, most appropriate, a pleasant surprise, or simply something that never occurred to me, I thank them (Professor Toney).

Show Enthusiasm

An overwhelming majority of these teachers are enthusiastic about their teaching and use that quality to convey the message to the student that something exciting is about to happen:

> When my car hits the parking lot, my adrenalin starts to flow and I come alive (Professor Reich).

> I'm enthusiastic and make it clear that *I like* what we're doing, the textbooks, the assignments, the objectives, learning, writing, reading, being in a classroom with them, etc. (Professor Skellings).

These examples typify the committed, enthusiastic instructors we recognize as excellent. They are consciously aware of their influence and of their ability to program success for their students by their actions. They believe in their own effectiveness. They know how to create success in students, and they reward that success when it appears. All the while, they maintain a cheerful, exciting image which provides a model of their enthusiasm for the students and entices them into the realm of success.

Reward Orientation

Excellent teachers love teaching. They are satisfied with their profession. Cohen and Brawer (1977) found a correlation between teachers who are concerned about students and those who have high job satisfaction. Despite the negative press that teaching has been getting for the past two decades, despite the long hours, low pay, and lack of recognition among the public for their contributions, excellent teachers enjoy their work. What is the inside story that is missed by the critics? What do teachers know about their jobs that makes them willing to put up with the frustrations of underprepared students, drug problems, student discipline problems, administrative bureaucracy, and lack of respect from members of other professions?

The answer is in the responses to their teaching that teachers receive daily. The nod of understanding, the delight experienced by a novice, their own feelings of achievement when a former student succeeds in his career field—these are the rewards of excellent teachers. They receive enormous satisfaction from seeing their work pay off. In few fields is the strain of work as intense or the rewards as personal.

Excellent teachers spend long hours preparing clear, concise presentations for the steering group, adaptations of the lesson for those with individual problems, and extra time after class reiterating their main points and providing direction to students in need. In turn, they receive, along with their paychecks, a bonus—the "psychic income" of seeing a student's face light up with understanding when he masters a new concept or learns a new skill (Futrell, 1984):

The bottom line is knowing that I might have made a positive difference in someone's life. Watching attitudes change and confidence increase is exciting. "Turning someone on" to mathematics and having him/her express appreciation is so very rewarding (Professor Gill).

Not only do teachers receive "strokes" when they see achievement in their classrooms, but these exceptional teachers also have ongoing relationships with students that provide them with positive feedback long after those students have graduated:

I feel great when my students succeed in class or in life. Sometimes it is because I am proud that I might presume to be part of the reason for the success. Sometimes it is because I am touched by how much the person wanted me to know about the success. ("I couldn't wait to tell you that I got a 7 on my essay on the CLAST exam!") Sometimes it is because I know the effort that was put forth to achieve the success. I am especially delighted by the success of students who made it against the odds (Professor Skellings).

This thrill is increased when teachers see former students who have applied their skills successfully in job situations:

I have been able through the years to encourage students to achieve at a very high level. I have had many students who have become researchers, physicians, or school administrators and teachers, and I have received many letters of thanks. One of my former students wrote a newspaper article thanking me for being the kind of teacher that I am (Professor Bateman).

The reward these teachers feel appears to be a major motivating force behind excellence in teaching. As teachers experience this stimulus, they begin to recycle the energy back to the student in the form of renewed commitment, higher expectations, an integrated perception of the subject and their students, and a positive attitude, including a vibrant sense of enthusiasm.

INTERPERSONAL THEMES

According to Klemp's system of categorizing, interpersonal themes are important components of a successful profile. The teaching themes of objectivity, active listening, rapport, and empathy fit comfortably under this general umbrella. Interest in these areas has blossomed.

Suddenly the bookstores are filled with literature on how to improve interpersonal skills, speakers are offering workshops at local high schools, and many businesses are hiring consultants to teach employees how to create more effective relationships. People have recently begun to recognize that interpersonal skills make a substantial contribution to the atmosphere of a work area.

Educators have long been aware of the impact of interpersonal skills in the classroom. Much has been written about the role of a congenial and supportive climate in learning. Easton et al. (1984) report that effective community college teachers "create a classroom atmosphere that they describe as relaxed, comfortable, cheerful, friendly, nonthreatening, and positive" (p. 8). More recently, research by Guskey and Easton (1983) in community colleges confirmed this finding. They make the case that teachers who show an interest in their students encourage students through that behavior to become involved, which in turn enhances their learning and achievement.

How is this learning environment established? Teachers have found that by learning the name of and a few facts about each student, they demonstrate to students that they are interested in them. Then excellent teachers use this information to relate the course materials to the interests, hobbies, and talents of the class members. They show concern over the difficulties and triumphs experienced in their classes and they share their own feelings with students to create a closer, shared experience. When they make a mistake, they admit it, thus demonstrating that "to err is human," and that mistakes can be tolerated and used as learning devices. These teachers also show a sensitivity to the student's background and try to use that background as a positive point of departure for dealing with the subject matter.

Showing interest and concern is significant, but it is equally important not to become so personal that the student feels harassed, violated, or embarrassed (Guskey & Easton, 1982). A supportive climate prevents emotional overload by defining personal decorum. By sharing personal feelings, the teacher encourages the student to open up. When students do contribute, their information is put into the context of the lesson. The student is thus shown appreciation for his involvement, and the exchange models for other students that opinions, thoughts, feelings, and interests are accepted and respected in the classroom. Often humor is used to show the student that learning does not have to be a dangerous risk. Corrective feedback is given in a nonthreatening, objective way.

A high-school study by Ware (1978) describes the kind of rewards that students prefer. They rejected most extrinsic types of rewards such as plaques, certificates, or public recognition. Their preference was for the intrinsic types of rewards that are difficult for school systems to implement. The top four choices were (1) reaching a personal goal; (2) receiving a scholarship for school; (3) getting compliments and encouragement from friends; and (4) being accepted as a person and having others seek their opinions. Some of these rewards can be structured into individual classrooms. Students in the survey suggested that teachers provide moral support, teach and encourage students to be more complimentary to one another, listen, encourage the sharing of successes, recognize individuals as worthwhile, and teach communication skills.

A number of studies at the secondary and college level document a dichotomy among teachers: some teachers foster good attitudes in students, while others foster learning potential (Good, Biddle, & Brophy, 1975). As one group of researchers remarked, "Satisfying human relationships is a necessary but insufficient condition for student learning" (Murphy, Weil, Hallinger, & Mitman, 1982). Creating an environment that is responsive to both these concerns is typical of intuitive teachers. They use their interpersonal skills to enhance learning outcomes. This section focuses on four interpersonal themes: objectivity, active listening, rapport, and empathy. Around these themes cluster specific characteristics used by excellent teachers to create a supportive climate conducive to effective learning.

OBJECTIVITY

Although college teachers are not faced with the discipline problems that high school teachers cope with, they still have to maintain a sense of fair play in dealing with classroom interaction. Sometimes students inadvertently offend others, act surly, or have disruptive mannerisms. In any of these situations, excellent teachers respond calmly and objectively (Coker, Medley, & Soar, 1980). They try to determine the facts; they do not seek to blame, but choose to solve the problem quickly and efficiently before it gets more complex.

Approach Students with Friendly, Business-Like Attitude

Exceptional teachers are patient and understanding, nurturing the positive in each student. However, they are task-oriented at the same time. They do not lose sight of their goals and the achievement focus, approaching their task in a business-like fashion that uses communication skills effectively to create involvement around their subject matter.

159

Evaluate Objectively and Fairly

Tough situations are handled calmly, with routine self-assurance. By keeping some distance between self and the problem, excellent teachers are better able to respond fairly:

> The best situation is to avoid "emotional" relationships. If one seems to be developing, I believe it is best to just listen—not to make any quick decisions or react in haste. Once things have "cooled down," I make an attempt to discuss the situation and evaluate the total issue (Professor Stokes).

> I remind myself that we all use defense mechanisms, and I attempt to put mine aside long enough to analyze the situation objectively. I encourage students to express themselves, but at the same time I remind them that most often "it's not *what* you say but *how* you say it." If we can agree to proceed from this point, it is usually possible to get all the issues on the table (Professor Ferguson).

Seek Solutions, Not Blame

These teachers concentrate on the solution, not on the blame. They are interested in getting on with the lesson; they expend only what energy is necessary to move the situation to a constructive close:

> Not long ago I had a student who repeatedly asked questions in class that went well beyond the range of the course content. I told him that his questions were good ones, but that many of them could not be entertained in class due to the nature of the course and time constraints. I invited him to visit me during my office hours. As it turned out, we had several good discussions on the subject over coffee (Professor Toney).

Side with the Student

The successful teachers whom we interviewed indicated that they feel they are on the student's side. This quality is also mentioned in the Chicago study on effective teaching in community colleges (Easton et al., 1984). Professor Weaver's comments are representative of the attitudes of successful teachers at Miami-Dade:

> I try to convey that my job is to help [students] discover some new things in what might be a challenging experience— that I am on their side on an exam—not the exam's side.

They try to understand individual behavior, learn the facts, and make objective decisions, yet all within the realm of the task at hand—learning the course material.

ACTIVE LISTENING

Attentive listening is a communication skill that is basic to effective interaction. We found that the teachers we studied are exceptionally committed to careful and distinct listening, that they repeat student responses to assure correct interpretation, and that they make use of nonverbal cues as well. Aspy (1973) describes these paraphrasings as interchangeable responses. Teachers use these interchangeable responses to summarize what the student has said (Good, Biddle, & Brophy, 1975). They are feedback intended not only to validate perceptions, but also to communicate that what the student has to say is valued. Both of these make the students feel they are worthwhile and that their thoughts are important.

Paraphrase for Clarification

Correlational studies (Good, Biddle, & Brophy, 1975) on interchangeable responses indicate that improved student gains are a direct result of interchangeable responses by the teachers, rather than of some extraneous variable. Paraphrasing also includes the acuity of the teacher in perceiving the nuances and implications of what the student is saying.

Take Time to Hear Student Out

The key to actually hearing one's students is to care first about what they say, and I definitely care. I want to know what they think—I want to hear their ideas and suggestions. I believe it is also important to provide an atmosphere in which good communication is possible and encouraged. In addition, one must take the time to listen and strive to provide time for student interaction (Professor Stokes).

Effective teachers can "listen" attentively on paper as well as in a classroom. Often they are required to read between the lines to determine exactly what the student is saying. Taking time to jot notes to students is another way of showing they care and that the student is important (Brown & Thornton, 1963). These small gestures are not lost on students; they help to create the relationship between teacher and student that has been related to student success in college (Wilson et al., 1975).

Attend to Nonverbal Clues

In a study by Schneider, Klemp, and Kastendiek (1981), many effective teachers described how they interpret individual nonverbal clues or read the mood of a group. Often by looking over the class, teachers can sense if they are explaining clearly, keeping students interested, and maintaining a pace that is appropriate. Professor Weaver has a succinct process for integrating nonverbal communication: "When in the classroom I watch their eyes! They speak volumes!" In a multiethnic setting like Miami-Dade, many of the nonverbal cues are also cultural and must be learned by faculty:

> I am careful to be respectful of students, never to refer to personal qualities such as physical appearance, accent, etc.; I am solicitous of health problems, alert to appearances of nervousness, sadness, etc. (Professor Cubbison).

Willing to Listen out of Class

Wilson et al. (1975) found that the biggest difference between effective teachers and others was the extent to which they are involved with students outside of class. Sometimes their motives are to try to reach the student in class by using out-of-class knowledge:

> I never discourage students who want to share personal feelings. This type of sharing often gives me insight as to the best approach to helping that student succeed (Professor Ferguson).

At other times, these successful teachers manifest the caring characteristic of teachers involved in close relationships with their students:

> I am flattered when a student feels open enough with me to share personal feelings. I am not trained in any counseling techniques, so I avoid giving advice unless I feel quite confident about what I am suggesting (Professor Rose).

> I want students to know that I am willing to listen. If I am conferring with a student over a personal problem, I elect to allow the student the opportunity to talk as much as possible. I do a great deal of listening and use a "non-directed" approach as much as I can. Often the student will arrive at a viable solution on his own (Professor Gill).

Excellent teachers really are excellent listeners.

RAPPORT

Rapport is a quality closely related to both active listening and empathy. We have defined it in our work as the ability to maintain an approving and mutually favorable relationship with students. Rapport is built between teacher and student, but is also fostered among students in order to create the unthreatening climate beneficial to a free exchange. Teachers express rapport not only through relationships, but also through humor, caring, and respect. Establishing good rapport with students requires that teachers be open and honest. Teachers who create high levels of rapport do so by openly exchanging information and feelings with students.

Research is clear about the importance of faculty-student interactions to the student's desire to stay in school and to benefit from what the college environment offers (Wilson et al., 1975). Easton et al. (1984) support the use of personal information to make classes more relevant to students. Another major study concludes that an essential characteristic of the most successful college professors is having rapport with students. A careful look at the facets of rapport will clarify these research findings.

Exhibit a Sense of Humor

Teachers create rapport with their use of humor (Ellner & Barnes, 1983). Teachers who exhibit a sense of humor appear more human and more accessible to students. Humor also creates a feeling that learning itself is fun, that the subject matter need not be intimidating:

> I see a very direct relation between having a good time in class, laughing in class, feeling comfortable in class, and being motivated to work hard, read more, prepare thoroughly, produce more, etc. (Professor Rose).

The connection between productivity and fun has yet to be borne out in the literature, but it is definitely a way of teaching that excellent teachers feel produces results in their students. This area warrants further investigation in order to establish whether the correlation between fun and learning really exists. It may cause a good feeling, a feeling of rapport, which in turn leads to the desire to excel, to perform, to do one's best. It does seem that if something is enjoyable, more time will be spent doing it. And time on task has been widely validated in the literature as a means to spurring achievement in a subject area (Stallings, 1981).

Show Personal Interest in Students

Active listening is only one way that teachers show a personal interest in students. Teachers who take the time to learn their students' names and some information about them can use this later to spark discussions relevant to subject material. Showing an interest in another is the first step in building a relationship. Good teachers foster relationships in the belief that learning will be enhanced. Some teachers incorporate this personal interest in students into an introductory procedure:

> Near the beginning of the term my students fill out a questionnaire for me so that I can get to know them a little better. Among the questions I ask are: What is your travel experience? What are your hobbies? What do you do in your leisure time? By remembering some of their responses and tying them in with the course I help them to have an identity and sense of importance (Professor Toney).

> I make eye contact with people in class, smile, nod, and do everything in my power to let them know that I am aware of their presence and am concerned about their academic needs. This is not always easy—I teach large lecture classes with 70–130 students (Professor Blitzer).

Establish Harmonious Relationships with Students

> I value my relationship with my students, and hope that many friendships, as well as teacher-student relationships, continue to develop (Professor Rose).

Some teachers describe rapport as the stuff that makes teaching another person possible. Without it they cannot work. The teacher-student relationship is carefully constructed to allow learning to take place. Many excellent teachers find ways of capturing student attention, and pleasant, friendly interaction helps:

> When I see my students outside of class and recognize them, I speak. If they are seated nearby at a ball game or in the cafeteria, etc., I often ask them to join me if it seems that it would not make them uncomfortable (Professor Toney).

> My interest in students' personal lives, my compliments to students on their dress and grooming, my inquiries about

absences, my use of humor and teasing are a few ways I think I try to establish harmonious relationships with my students. I especially find it enlightening to speak to them in the halls or after class to elicit feedback on a one-to-one basis (Professor Reich).

Professor Reich takes time to notice them, to establish a presence in their lives, to let them know she cares about them and wants them to be open with her in return. She builds a trust that will later be useful when introducing new material or asking for a new behavior. These relationships are well worth the time they take to build because they become springboards for later demands.

Show Students Respect

Showing students respect is another aspect of creating rapport. Respect lets students know that they are valued and that the professor really accepts them as equals in being, if not in knowing:

I usually call them "Miss X" or "Mr. Y" in order to show that I regard them as mature individuals. I always liked that when I was in college (Professor Cubbison).

When students feel respected, it increases their learning capabilities. They are willing to ask questions or come to the office for help. They are willing to devote time to learn the subject (Professor Sanchez).

Create Caring Climate in Classroom

A supportive climate is a strong component of rapport. Within a protective environment, students are free to express themselves, to build trusting relationships with their professors and with each other:

I create a classroom atmosphere that is non-threatening to the student's relationship with me and with other students. The student might well be threatened by a pop quiz or a major test if he hasn't studied, but I do not want him to be threatened by the thought that I might embarrass him or put him on the spot. If a student tells me that he is ill at ease about being called on in class, I honor that. I want my classroom to be a place where people feel comfortable, accepted (Professor Rose).

Climate is established according to the professor's values:

> A structured, attentive, polite, and respectful atmosphere permits humorous remarks, spontaneous comments, disagreement about interpretations, etc., to occur from all of us without letting the classroom degenerate into chaos (Professor Cubbison).

Excellent teachers know the value of establishing open and supportive climates in their classrooms.

EMPATHY

Empathy is the ability to stand in another's shoes, to understand reality from another's perspective. This quality evokes a deep response in one person for another. Superior teachers are warm and caring, yet they assert high expectations firmly and fairly by laying well-planned paths to success for their students.

Model Caring Behavior

Excellent teachers are often empathetic and reach out to students in need. By showing them that they feel for the students in their particular situation, they model caring behavior. Some of the attributes of active listening are shared with empathy, such as this recognition of another's feelings.

Share Self with the Class

Similar to modeling, effective teachers demonstrate how to induce empathy by sharing their own feelings with the class. A teacher may lessen students' fear of failure by revealing his or her own flaws:

> I want people to be able to learn abstract, complex logic in an informal, comfortable, supportive environment. To this end I share my own difficulties when I first encountered the material (Professor Blitzer).

> Students need to know that their professors are human beings who have faced and conquered the same challenges that they face. Moreover, they seem to get encouragement from the knowledge that teachers still face daily challenges (Professor Ferguson).

Demonstrate Understanding of Others

The ability to understand others and to demonstrate that understanding are special qualities, and the outstanding teachers in our study possess those qualities:

Sometimes students have severe problems which are very emotional for them. I am very empathetic in response to these problems. I am also a touching person, so a pat on the back or a hug often helps (Professor Bateman).

Excellent teachers never forget what they are about. They use emotions to get at their teaching mission, but the emotions are not substitutes for the teaching-learning process.

The interpersonal qualities of objectivity, active listening, rapport, and empathy suggest that successful people are people-oriented. We know (from Klemp, 1977) that successful people have well-developed interpersonal skills; excellent professors are no different. They show what Klemp calls "active empathy," being able to pick up and act on clues conveyed by others. Interpreting signals correctly enables teachers to help students overcome their problems, which in turn facilitates learning. Effective teachers evaluate objectively, exercising fairness in their judgments. They listen carefully to what is being said, ever mindful of the person behind the words, and make themselves available for personal exchanges. The best teachers have learned to use humor, personal interests, and respect to help establish meaningful relationships with students, and they create climates conducive to sharing and feelings of trust. And finally, they know how to express the care they feel for others who are in awkward or painful situations.

INTELLECTUAL THEMES

In addition to motivation and interpersonal skills, exceptional teachers use another group of skills and characteristics to propagate their trade. This final group of characteristics considered in our study, the intellectual themes, includes an individualized perception of students, use of teaching strategies, knowledge, and innovation. In adopting the Klemp model (1977), we agreed that intellectual or cognitive skills involve the ability to synthesize information thematically and logically, to understand many sides of a controversial issue, and to learn from experience. In the last two sections, we have explained *how* excellent teachers teach; in this section we investigate *what* they teach.

INDIVIDUALIZED PERCEPTION

Seeing students as individuals with different learning styles, different interests, and different motivations is what is meant by individualized perception. Wilson et al. (1975) point out that students want to learn different things, according to their interests. These authors acknowledge that there are many methods now in use to help instructors individualize, such as mastery learning, self-paced learning, and personalized systems of instruction.

Students may be the best sources of how they learn and how a course can best serve their needs (McKeachie, 1978). This innovative idea seems foreign to many educators, but as qualitative research has shown, there is merit in going directly to the source for information. Easton et al. (1984) affirm that effective teachers use personal information to adjust coursework to individual needs. Exemplary teachers also recognize individual efforts to reach the goal, whether the person meets with total success or only partial success. Rewarding desired behaviors is one way to help ensure such outcomes.

See Students As Individuals

Being able to understand individual needs in a crowded classroom is tough work. It requires someone with insight, caring, an ability to draw out needs, and an adaptive attitude. Excellent teachers do not teach the subject; they teach the student. They know how to introduce a general subject, call for questions, and then make adaptations to their lessons as necessary to serve that particular group.

Professor Jim Gray views students as "individuals who want to learn about the subjects I teach. In many cases, I view myself more as a mentor than a traditional teacher." The idea of being a mentor lends itself to individualization. Because he believes that students gain from personal guidance, Professor Gray prepares his instruction so that all applications will be based on the individual needs of his students.

Although teachers have specific standards they wish to meet and specific material they intend to cover, they realize that each student may approach those goals in a different manner, and they respect differences as valuable. Professor Stokes explains,

> I try to accommodate each individual by accepting each individual for what and who he or she is. I encourage each to reach his potential by doing his best, and I do not compare students.

Some subjects lend themselves to this ideology better than others. But just as it is possible to maintain eye contact in a lecture class of 130 students, it is possible to maintain an individualized perspective if that is the goal of the teacher.

Adjust Courses to Individual Needs

Coursework can be adjusted to accommodate student differences. For example, handicapped students may require remedial adaptations. Differences in culture, philosophy, and outlook may suggest another set of adjustments or accommodations. Often teachers make allowances for personal setbacks or external contingencies, such as illness, family problems, or learning disabilities:

> I meet regularly in my office with any LD [learning disabled] student, in order to try to find workable methods for that particular student and to see if that student has suggestions for me based on previous special education instruction that he has received (Professor Rose).

> We have a great variety of learning abilities. I have several extra credit assignments and projects for the more able students. I also use these more advanced students as peer leaders in the business lab to help the slower learners (Professor Gray).

Meeting personal needs is not easy; it requires conscientious effort, even when the teacher is motivated to do it, but great teachers care enough to individualize.

Recognize Effort

Many people imagine that the best teachers teach the best students and that is why they are so successful. Miami-Dade Community College serves some of the poorest, some of the most deprived groups in the country, with many foreign, minority, and refugee students. It has a solid core of typical middle-class students as well. But no one can say that the excellent teachers at Miami-Dade are excellent because they have an elite student body. In fact, few of the teachers we interviewed failed to say that they enjoyed this diversity or the challenge of working with such a variety of students. The teachers we interviewed confirmed that the diversity demands they reward effort as well as achievement, ever mindful that the achievement will eventually come:

> I try to use as many ways as possible to let students know they have given a good effort. I will comment to them in class, write comments on their papers, and in general encourage them to continue to give their good effort (Professor Stokes).

Students respond well to the effort their teachers make to reward them, to provide for their individual differences, and to appreciate their individuality. These teachers make success a reality for students.

TEACHING STRATEGIES

The point of teaching is to activate students to think, to learn, to apply, to evaluate, to synthesize, and finally, to grow. Teachers accomplish these ends through six major strategies: well-organized courses, student involvement, higher-order thinking skills, relevancy of application, use of monitoring and evaluation, and flexibility and variety in delivery.

The way courses are structured varies with each professor. But each excellent teacher carefully structures his or her material from simple to complex as each new idea is introduced, so that student success is built into the action plan. The goal of student accomplishment acts as a beacon in the teachers' planning; everything they do is to further the progress of students toward achievement. Professors have been known to growl that students do not belong in their classes, that they don't have the background (Elbe, 1976). But the excellent teachers we studied do not complain that their students don't know enough. They fully accept the responsibility of teaching students what they need to know about a certain portion of a subject area.

These professionals carefully organize their courses, making each class a necessary step in the total structure. Although the jury is still out on the validity of student-centeredness (using student input as the center of the curriculum), there is agreement that actively involving students facilitates learning (McKeachie, 1978).

Helping students extend their thinking to new dimensions is another way to move students toward achievement. Excellent teachers suggest applications of the information or skills that they are sharing in interesting and relevant ways. Evaluation reinforces learning and provides a means to monitor the progress of students. Effective teachers carefully plan and execute lessons that add to the content of the course, but they maintain flexibility so that they can be responsive to the daily needs of their students.

Offer Well-Organized Courses and Classes

Brown and Thornton (1963) reveal, in their research on effectiveness, that clear standards of performance should be included in the course syllabus. Effective teachers work hard. They take time to prepare lessons that put across their messages with a punch. They carefully break down what needs to be mastered into small doses that can be fed to students bit by bit. They do not use their knowledge to impress or intimidate students, but carefully reveal it so that it is not overwhelming to novices. They tailor "a well-controlled, well-organized situation, where the students can perceive a direction and purpose for each class" (Professor Rose).

> I use precise and understandable definitions of new ideas and concepts. I write them on the blackboard and allow for class discussion. Mathematics is a language, and students should learn the terminology used in mathematics to be able to understand the questions and the textbook (Professor Sanchez).

From the beginning of the semester, these teachers are clear about their demands and expectations of students:

> I give them a sheet of general instructions telling all the dates of importance, general rules of the games, etc. I give them a course syllabus telling which topics and chapters we will be covering. I also give them a separate sheet covering how to write up the reports I require, all in an attempt to make them understand what is expected of them and to have no fear or surprises (Professor Huff).

From start to finish, courses with these teachers are clear, concise, and sequential so that students can reach the required standards.

Get Students Involved

Student riots in Paris traditionally have centered around the lack of involvement allowed students at the Sorbonne. Sitting passively while a monotonous professor drones on has had little appeal to students for centuries. Easton et al. (1984) concur that effective teachers know how to engage student attention and involvement. They find a multitude of strategies to engage students in their own learning:

> In the last few years I have been insisting that students bring their own texts with them to class, and rather than using the overhead projector, I refer them to the text photographs, illustrations, charts, and diagrams. It seems to be working; they are apparently just a little more involved (Professor Toney).

I design many opportunities for students to manipulate the new information they are acquiring. This is in the form of "hands on" lab work, lots of quizzes and checks, and citing relevant newspaper and television material (Professor Weaver).

Oral exercises are done in class frequently. I use a "round robin" approach to insure maximum individual participation. This approach helps in identifying individual needs and allows for immediate feedback (Professor Ferguson).

Encourage Higher-Order Thinking

Teachers with high expectations have high standards as well. They want students to learn to think, not just to master by rote sets of facts. According to Ellner and Barnes (1983), the purpose of some courses is to develop "higher-order thinking skills and cognitive structures" in students. To this end, superior teachers program learning activities which facilitate creative thought. Questioning techniques are most common in this regard:

I use Bloom's Taxonomy of Educational Objectives (I. knowing, II. comprehending, III. applying, IV. analyzing, V. synthesizing, VI. evaluating) as a guide to developing appropriate objectives for each class. These action levels of cognitive behavior also prove useful in guiding the slower students through the necessary steps to bring them up to the level of expectation for a given course (Professor Ferguson).

Using a similar technique, Candido Sanchez gives examples to his natural science students that slowly increase in level of difficulty. Drawing students out of their present thinking patterns into more complex ones takes a structured approach, a well-thought-out plan of attack. But it certainly is an appropriate behavior among college faculty, and the teachers we studied were no exception:

I ask them questions, knowing that their answers teach them more than I can (Professor Weaver).

Higher order thinking is enhanced by bringing in occasional lapses in critical thinking from newspapers, and by analyzing anti-learning in popular culture—what mass audiences are expected to believe is a satisfactory resolution to a serious problem but which is in actuality avoidance of the issue (Professor Altshuler).

I encourage and reward students for creativity in problem solving (Professor Gill).

Colleges, particularly those with heavy liberal arts commitments, are interested in teaching people to think. It is part of the mission of higher education to propagate innovative thinking. It should be no surprise that community college teachers reward high-level thinking skills.

Make Coursework Relevant

Excellent teachers believe that students are more likely to participate when the material is connected to their personal lives, and they make these connections by bringing in practical applications (Easton, 1984). Wilson et al. (1975) found that more effective teachers use analogies to illustrate their lessons and share examples from their own experiences or research. The literature is clear on the virtue of making coursework relevant (Bruner, 1960). Students who understand *why* they are learning are more motivated to learn:

> As I see it, the key to making the subject relevant is to first understand my students. I try to find out about them, their interests and needs, and then relate what is learned to this (Professor Stokes).

Monitor Student Progress

Monitoring, or keeping track of where students are in terms of the goal, is a key ingredient to success. Active teachers vigilantly keep abreast of student progress and use pop quizzes and homework to assure steady movement toward course goals. They give fair tests that assess what they are teaching (Wotruba & Wright, 1975). Many teachers teach in general terms (high inference) and then expect students to apply the material at specific levels (low inference), without having made any transitions in thinking for the students to make the connection (Borich, 1982). For example, a teacher explains what an astronaut is but expects the students to know how to train one. This high inference-low inference dilemma may occur often, but effective teachers avoid it by consciously helping students see relationships between concepts or between questions and concepts.

Excellent teachers understand that testing is a way of reinforcing learning. They construct test items which will build on class skills and use higher-order thinking skills, but only in the context of the material that has actually been covered:

> I privately review exams to be sure that the material is either in the text or was covered in class (Professor Toney).

> In the teaching of mathematics I take little for granted in terms of background and constantly review and reinforce.... By constructing fair and reasonable examinations, I give students an opportunity to experience success (Professor Jack Gill).

Other aspects of monitoring include keeping students moving at an appropriate pace, following up on homework assignments, and giving quizzes to review and strengthen learning.

Monitoring is essential to keep students attuned to their progress. Providing feedback has been cited in the literature as a major monitoring strategy (Easton, 1984).

> In teaching composition, I have part of most assignments written at home by the student, and part written in class. This assures me that students are doing their own writing, and it gives me the chance to intervene and make corrections and suggestions as they are in the process of writing. I also make some use of peer evaluation (Professor Rose).

Feedback, whether oral or written, establishes communication between teacher and learner on the attainment of course goals:

> I give students as much feedback as possible, verbally and by writing messages on their papers (Professor Stokes).

Show Flexibility in Planning and Delivery

Exceptional teachers use a variety of delivery systems (Billips & Rauth, 1984). They alternate lectures, discussion, and audiovisual stimuli with student presentations, guest lecturers, and field trips. The teacher chooses the appropriate method of presentation with the objectives, content, and student group in mind:

> I try to structure the course so that there is a wide variety of ways a student's success can be measured, not by tests alone (Professor Huff).

Effective teachers are ready for contingencies, and although unplanned activities may be disruptive, these teachers try to incorporate them into the lesson. They carefully plan the major points, but remain flexible about their delivery strategies. These teachers do not neglect factors such as the time of day the course is taught:

My strategies include lectures, demonstrations, questions and answers, and examples. The mix of these will depend on the hour of the day the class is taught or the course being taught. A 9:00 a.m. section is taught much differently from a 5:30 p.m. class because of the differences in student population and their alertness. Each section demands its own strategy, and this I play by ear (Professor Gray).

KNOWLEDGE

Knowledge is a process, not a product. Effective teachers, although knowledgeable in their subject matter and in teaching strategies, understand that they are lifelong learners. They enjoy learning and find opportunities to share learning experiences often. They are avid readers and especially enjoy finding out from one another what techniques work best. They participate in workshops, conferences, national teaching groups, and inservice development. They also use their own study to model for students the importance of education and the value that it holds for them personally.

Know Subject Matter

Knowing one's subject is a crucial characteristic of a superb teacher (Wotruba & Wright, 1975). However, knowing a subject well appears to be so fundamental a quality that little explanation of it is given in the literature. We will assume for this study that it can be partially assessed by the recognition of others and in scholarly activities in the field:

> I develop curriculum for my department. Some of the material being used by my department as the central text has been written by me. I am under contract to Prentice-Hall to write four books in the area of English for Special Purposes (Professor Welch).

> I recently had two books published, *College Math Review* and *Competency in College Mathematics*. I'm currently working on an algebra series (Professor Blitzer).

Enjoy Learning

We found that effective teachers love to learn. They take other people's classes, read, write, bring in examples of things they have learned for their students, and genuinely take pleasure in adding to their store of knowledge:

When I learn something in front of students (this happens often), I'm sure to make a big deal of it, honestly and sincerely expressing my pleasure over the whole experience. I push learning and expound upon my ideas concerning the joy of lifelong learning (Professor Toney).

Engage in Professional Development

The teachers we studied are continually involved in upgrading their knowledge in their teaching fields. They enjoy swapping "techniques" on how to teach, as well:

I periodically take courses to refresh and update my knowledge and to remain abreast of new trends in mathematics education. I hold memberships in several state and national organizations. This keeps me constantly in touch with new ideas (Professor Gill).

I read journals, go to conferences and conventions in my field, take courses in or out of my field (I'm taking aerobics right now and learning a lot from the P.E. teacher), do projects which enable me to talk to teachers in other areas and see what it's like to be a student and to learn (Professor Skellings).

The excitement in learning expressed by excellent teachers differs somewhat from the attitude of other teachers in a study by Schneider, Klemp, and Kastendiek (1981): "While the average faculty members espoused an appreciation for humanistic education, virtually none described themselves as directly engaged in remedial learning [as did the effective teachers]." Our study affirms the zeal that excellent teachers bring to the process of learning.

INNOVATION

Literature on improving college teaching through innovation mentions Miami-Dade Community College as a leader in terms of setting up a faculty and professional development center (Wilson, 1975). These centers have now become fixtures on many campuses and are easily accessible resources for teachers searching for information on how to change their teaching style or how to find a new method to introduce a concept. In addition, mini-grants are offered to teachers with new ideas that require some resources to get going. Creative educators have put money behind the ideas they feel are important.

The successful teachers we studied at Miami-Dade enjoy putting spice into their teaching. They integrate new ideas in a planned, deliberate way. They search for new and current information, and they are willing to take risks in the hope that one of their innovations will pay off.

Integrate New Ideas

Most teachers try something new at least once in a while. Excellent teachers probably are more thoughtful in how they integrate new ideas into their routines. They carefully pilot a new strategy, working out the bugs in one class before they adapt it wholeheartedly:

> Most new ideas have been around in other guises. Some ideas work for a particular group of people or at a particular time or some combination of those two. In order to reach as many students as possible, one must experiment and change. In general I've had fair success with new ideas, which are undoubtedly someone else's old ideas (Professor Weaver).

> I probably abandon more than half of the new ideas that I try after one or two attempts. But, because new ideas often represent growth, I try to keep my mind open (Professor Toney).

Search for New Strategies

These excellent teachers read journals, talk to other teachers, take others' classes, and actively hunt for new information, techniques, or equipment for the sole purpose of improving their teaching. They are eager to find ways to facilitate learning:

> My teaching is a composite of new ideas. The effective ones I retain term in and term out. Those that fall flat (and many do) are either modified or retired. This results in fresh course content. I am never bored with or tired of the same old thing (Professor Reich).

> I like variety, and students seem to respond. I usually have to give a new approach two or three tries before I can determine if it fits my basic style. Generally, I have good results (Professor Ferguson).

Take Risks to Improve Curriculum

Psychologists often describe teachers as preferring the known, stable element, not as risk-takers. In our study we found that excellent teachers are quite willing to reach out to a new idea, especially if it will improve student achievement:

> I could not stand it if I did not try new ideas. I keep looking for and thinking of different ways to present material. Results are excellent. Each year I become more effective (Professor Bateman).

> I have no hesitation in trying new ideas. I know I can learn from others. I have incorporated several ideas of my colleagues into my own teaching strategies. Generally, the results are good (Professor Gill).

The results of our study on excellent teachers show that at least some of them prefer to take risks. The best are not seeking a secure profession; they enjoy the pizzazz of novelty, as long as it leads to improvements in their own competency.

SUMMARY

Our study validates much of the previous literature on excellence in teaching. There are several qualities not widely researched that we found and suggest may be distinguishing characteristics of exceptional teachers. First, the positive spirit with which these individuals attack their teaching is inspirational. They are "up," happy, satisfied individuals who do not allow "down" feelings to dampen classroom interaction. They leave their problems behind when they enter the classroom, and they give full, positive attention to their students.

Second, rewards for successful teachers are powerful motivators for continued interaction with students. The literature is scant on the importance of this trait, although there does seem to be recognition that exceptional teachers are satisfied in their jobs. It is our belief that success is such an enormous source of energy that it cannot be generalized by the term *satisfaction*. It is as if a cycle were created: each student success rewards the teacher, who in turn is energized to structure another opportunity for student success, and so the wheel spins.

Third, innovation, while heretofore not solidly linked with excellence in teaching, is a common characteristic of successful teachers. Superior teachers frequently mention risk-taking behavior in their instructional experimentation. The desire to try something new is an essential quality in truly creative people, and we encourage examination of this trait in exceptional teachers.

Our descriptive categorical study of superior teachers documents that teachers find powerful motivation in their deep- felt commitment, in the goals they set for themselves and their students, in the supportive attitude they bring to their teaching, in the integrated perception of both the students and their subject matter, and in the rewards that they receive from experiencing success with a student. They have refined their interpersonal skills to include an objective sense of fair play, an ability to listen and respond, a need to establish rapport with students, and an ability to demonstrate caring in warm, empathetic behaviors. Successful teachers also have well-developed intellectual skills. They value individualizing for personal accomplishment, they use effective teaching strategies, and they love learning and actively try to experiment with new ideas.

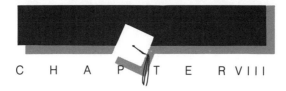

SUMMARY: THE EMERGENCE OF A NEW CULTURE

In this volume, we have described a community college which was designated an exemplar by a nationally representative group of professionals who have dedicated their careers to the development and improvement of community college teaching. The picture we have presented is only a snapshot of a complex, moving image—an action shot—because this archetypical institution continues to metamorphose and to move in new directions even as we compose these final comments. But this dynamic quality is to a large degree what makes Miami-Dade Community College a successful institution. Yet even as it continues to grow and transform itself, the college rests on a firm foundation. A number of researchers and writers define this foundation of basic assumptions and beliefs as the culture of an organization (Schein, 1985).

According to Schein, an organization's culture is a learned product which develops over time, resulting in a shared view and collective agreement on the correct way to perceive, think, and feel in relation to problems of external adaptation and internal integration. Eventually, culture evolves into an intrinsic, subtle phenomenon, essentially disappearing from the realm of explicit awareness. Schein views the basic model of culture formation as a matter of leaders consciously embedding culture by proposing solutions to problems the members of the organization face. If these solutions work continually, eventually they will be taken for granted, become unconscious assumptions, and finally will be taught to new members.

The precedent of innovation introduced by the founding president of Miami-Dade, Dr. Peter Masiko, established values and practices which set the stage for the shared culture now existing at the college. As Schein argues, the initial ability to share involves prior cultural learning and understanding, but new shared experience begins the formation of a new culture which becomes characteristic of that particular group of people. As with the reform process led by Dr. Robert McCabe, successor to Dr. Masiko and Miami-Dade's current president, the members of the work force at Miami-Dade simultaneously faced a problematic situation and worked out solutions together and, thus, transformed the original culture into the present one. During this formation

183

of a new culture, the employees as a group experienced learning every step of the way which resulted in shared values and beliefs which by now are ingrained and, to a large extent, unconscious and practically second nature to organizational members. Thus, the culture found today at Miami-Dade has evolved over time, spearheaded by strong leaders who have employed specific mechanisms which enable present members of the organization to accept and new members to adopt "the way things are done" at the college in order to meet the needs of an extremely diverse student population.

Schein (1985) has defined the techniques that leaders employ to develop organizational culture as "embedding mechanisms" which are methods of instilling values and assumptions in the employees of the organization. The information we have collected in our study of Miami-Dade includes strong evidence that President McCabe and his Executive Management Team have indeed embedded culture in the sense Schein describes by proposing solutions to problems the institution has faced. Only because these solutions have continued to work over time have the practices, policies, and mission become unconscious elements of the culture taken for granted by the inhabitants of the organization and taught to newcomers. That is, only elements that solve group problems will survive (Schein, 1985).

An important aspect of culture building should be noted. In order to embed a cultural element, a belief, or assumption, the leader must possess the ability to motivate the group to try out certain proposals and actions (Schein, 1983). Therefore, the creation of culture and the embedding of cultural elements have to be viewed simultaneously as a learning and teaching process (Schein, 1985). Thus, in the development of an organization, a leader must advocate persistently and hold tenaciously to his or her basic beliefs and values. The evidence is overwhelming that this is exactly what President McCabe and the people at Miami-Dade have done in achieving open admissions and high academic standards.

How President McCabe and his collaborators actually went about creating the cultural milieu responsible for formulating the pathway to the successes at Miami-Dade can be summarized in part by the five primary embedding mechanisms defined by Schein (1985): (1) what leaders pay attention to, measure, and control; (2) their reactions to critical incidents and organizational crises; (3) what they deliberately role model, what they teach, and how they coach; (4) the criteria they use for allocation of rewards and status; and, finally, (5) the criteria they use for recruitment, selection, promotion, retirement, and excommunication. Hence, what leaders pay attention to, react emotionally to, model, reward and punish, and select are the most powerful mechanisms that a leader has for embedding culture. Clearly the descriptive data presented throughout this volume substantiate the presence of these potent culture-embedding mechanisms.

According to Schein (1985), five additional mechanisms are used by leaders to communicate cultural messages. These embedding techniques are also readily apparent in the behaviors which have been enacted by leaders over time at Miami-Dade: (6) the organization's design and structure; (7) the systems and procedures; (8) the design of physical space, facades, and buildings; (9) the stories, legends, myths, and parables about important events and people; and (10) the formal statements of organizational philosophy, creeds, and charters. The systems and programs at Miami-Dade reinforce the cultural assumptions of caring about students and generating progress among a diverse student population. The cultural messages from the leaders at Miami-Dade are clear and consistent, resulting in unity of purpose and direction for the institution.

As current leadership theory contends, leadership is an interactional process in which followers often influence the leader as much as the leaders influence the followers. The Roueche-Baker Model of Community College Excellence (Figure 1) attempts to depict this interactional quality of leadership by presenting five organizational components which coexist in a dynamic state: (1) the college climate (a product of culture); (2) leadership attributes; (3) teaching qualities; (4) systems and programs; and (5) outcomes for students.

A comparison of the leadership attributes and teacher qualities which best describe the subjects studied in our investigation and which appear indicative of these components throughout the institution reveals striking similarities. Because, as authors on leadership contend, leadership is a process of inculcating values, attitudes, attributes, and behaviors in followers in an interactional fashion, teachers are able to bring about the same development of commitment in their students that organizational leaders do in members of the organization. That is, the qualities of both effective administrators and effective teachers are remarkably similar.

We have found from our studies of both public school and Miami-Dade that teachers, in fact, are leaders within the context of their own environment because they too inculcate attitude-shaping values, traits, and qualities. The human skills possessed by the Miami-Dade professors we interviewed are really what appear to set them apart—the ability

185

to motivate and inspire achievement in others. Both the administrators and professors who participated in the study were described by others as inspirational people. Almost always this type of evidence implies the quality of integrity, the quality of concern, and the quality of care about the well-being of individuals. The teacher in the classroom who cares about students is going to have tremendous influence on them because people respond to individuals who express sincere concern for them. In turn, administrators who sincerely care about the employees in the institution are going to influence the responses and motivations of organizational members in an extremely positive manner.

From strong leadership exercised by both the administration and the faculty of Miami-Dade, measurable student success has resulted. The efforts of all employees and of members of the community over the past decade have led to the creation of systems and programs which have produced improved student performance as indicated in higher completion rates and grade-point averages. Since the reforms have been put into place at the college, scores on the state college skills assessment exam, CLAST, have increased every term. In fact, Miami-Dade students earn higher scores than do students from the local universities which have admission standards. Suspension rates are down. The college reports increased success with students who are significantly underprepared when they enter college. Thus, the findings of our case study suggest (1) that directive and supportive systems, coupled with excellent performance—on the part of administration, staff, and faculty—lead to student success, and (2) that the leadership will continue to provide quality and equity in a motivating and dynamic environment.

Hence, the Roueche-Baker Model attempts to depict visually how a climate for excellence is directly related to the behaviors of the administrators and the qualities of the teachers and to the resultant systems—all of which depend upon a dedicated and loyal support staff. Furthermore, our model presents the way in which leadership influences behavior throughout the organization toward the development of successful systems, how these systems provide information about students, and how the staff by using the information manages students in such a way as to enhance exceptional teaching. All of these components aid in the development of a culture designed to ensure student success by encouraging effort, performance, and satisfaction along the pathway to student goals.

The success at Miami-Dade began with an organizational willingness to scrutinize reality and then to admit that things just were not as they should have been. Even while many insisted at the time that what was happening at the college was fine—that students should choose freely among courses and, in a phrase, have a "right to fail"—President McCabe could not accept the discrepancies in what was then the status quo. He saw that the educational system in general as well as the curricula at Miami-Dade did not match the needs of society. Recognizing that the very nature of work was changing and required a much higher level of skills than previously needed, President McCabe believed in the early 1970s, and believes today, that the college would not survive without the changes induced by the reform process. Essential to his commitment was the concept of open access, which for him is fundamental to the well-being of the country. Thus, he began his campaign for reform with the premise and gradually convinced others that students were *valued* by the institution. A three-year study and three years of interaction with the community and the staff, referred to by at least one staff member as "the war," convinced most people of the critical importance of the changes which had to be made in order to prepare students for the demands of contemporary society, a society quite different from that of the past. For President McCabe and the Miami-Dade staff, simply returning to the "good old days" was wrong—they believed education had to be better.

In this study, we have concluded that the unwavering commitment exhibited by Dr. McCabe and the people at Miami-Dade throughout an extremely taxing process was the key to their success. In other words, establishing the basic mission and philosophy and sticking to it contributes more to improving a situation than factors such as how much money is available or how conducive one setting is compared to another in achieving excellence. This conclusion was also borne out in our study of public schools. Excellence resides where there is commitment and support, whether in large or small schools, in urban or rural schools, or in schools with high or low socio-economic status. Probably no other community college in the world faces the student diversity that Miami-Dade does. It has the largest foreign nation representation and the largest foreign student enrollment of any community college. It has more minority students than any other college in Florida. Hence, if "input" is considered, no college has a more difficult chore in terms of attempting to meet the needs and to identify and correct the academic deficiencies of its learners than does Miami-Dade. Yet, this college has made an overwhelming difference, demonstrating that access and excellence can be achieved.

In beginning the reforms, President McCabe made four-decisions, to which he still adheres: (1) open access had to be maintained,

187

(2) if access were to be achieved, the college had to be much more directive, (3) the college had to be more supportive, and, finally, (4) high academic standards had to be maintained. These are the four principles upon which the success of the reforms at Miami-Dade rests.

In our study, we set out to discover, analyze, and evaluate an exemplary community college. We intended to document how climate, leadership, systems, and teaching can be synthesized to produce educational excellence. At Miami-Dade we found a culture which stands for excellence. This culture has been developed and learned over time. We determined that leaders in the college pay attention to student success and that computerized systems provide information in order that college personnel can make decisions for and with students to encourage achievement. We also determined that leaders react well to critical incidents and attempt to minimize crises and surprises. We discovered that leaders attempt to become role-models for excellence and that considerable teaching and coaching is occurring as college personnel attempt to improve performance. We also determined that the college has outstanding professors who are dedicated to good teaching and to helping their students succeed. We further discovered that the college is actively increasing rewards for, and positive expectations of, all personnel. Finally, we discovered that college personnel use current information in an effective way to assist in charting a path toward the future.

Perhaps most important, we found that people make the difference in achieving exemplary status for an institution. Excellent teaching thrives best in an environment which supports and fosters shared values focused on the central purpose of learning. Taken together, specific attitudes, approaches, policies, and decisions produce an achievement-oriented climate which is conducive to success among students and to high morale among staff. The evidence is convincing that at Miami-Dade students are truly valued and that the five components—climate, leadership, teaching, systems, and student outcomes—work synergistically to produce motivation and satisfaction among the people who work there and measurable growth and development for learners.

REFERENCES

Allman, T.D. (1983, February). The city of the future. *Esquire*, pp. 39–47.

Anandam, K. (1981, May). *Promises to keep...academic alert and advisement*. Miami: Miami-Dade Community College.

Aspy, D. (1973). A discussion of the relationship between selected student behavior and the teacher's use of interchangeable responses. Paper presented at AERA, New Orleans, LA.

Baker, G.A. III (1985). National Conference on Teaching Excellence. The University of Texas, Austin, TX.

Baldwin, A. (1984, September). *A comparative graduate profile for Miami-Dade Community College: 1982–83 and 1983–84*. (Research Report No. 84–24). Miami: Miami-Dade Community College.

Belcher, M. (1984a, July). *A cohort analysis of the relationship between entering basic skills and CLAST performance for all 1981 first-time-in-college students*. (Research Report No. 84–22). Miami: Miami-Dade Community College.

Belcher, M. (1984b, July). *Initial transcript analysis for a sample of students who failed two or more sections versus a sample who passed all four sections of the June 1984 CLAST*. (Research Report No. 84–21). Miami: Miami-Dade Community College.

Belcher, M. (1985a, February). *The role of developmental courses in improving CLAST performance*. (Research Report No. 85–04). Miami: Miami-Dade Community College.

Belcher, M. (1985b, March). *The general education mathematics curriculum and the CLAST*. (Research Report No. 85–12). Miami: Miami-Dade Community College.

Belcher, M. (1985c, May 3). Are improved CLAST scores due to higher entering basic skills scores of students taking the CLAST? Memorandum to Academic Affairs Committee, Research and Testing Committee, and Student Services Committee of Miami-Dade Community College.

Belcher, M., & Losak, J. (1985, April). *Providing educational opportunity for students who were initially ineligible to enroll in the state university* system. (Research Report No. 85–15). Miami: Miami-Dade Community College.

Billips, L.H., & Rauth, M. (1984). The new research: How effective teachers teach. *American Educator, 8,* 34–39.

Bogue, J.P. (1950). *The community college.* New York: McGraw-Hill.

Borich, G.D. (1982). *Review notes: evaluation models and techniques.* Austin, TX: The University of Texas.

Bowers, D.G. (1973). Organizational development techniques and their results in 23 organizations: The Michigan ICL study. *Journal of Applied Behavioral Science, 9,* 21–43.

Brown, D.G. (1979). *Leadership vitality: A workbook for academic administrators.* Washington, DC: American Council on Education.

Brown, J.W., & Thornton, J.W. (1963). *College teaching: Perspectives and guidelines.* New York: McGraw-Hill.

Bruner, J. (1960). *The process of education.* Cambridge, MA: Harvard University Press.

Campbell, J.P.; Dunnette, M.D.; Lawler, E.E.; & Weick, K.E. (1970). *Managerial behavior, performance, and effectiveness.* New York: McGraw-Hill.

Centra, J. (1979). *Determining faculty effectiveness.* San Francisco: Jossey-Bass.

Clark, B.R. (1960). *The open door college: A case study.* New York: McGraw-Hill.

Cohen, A.M., & Brawer, F.B. (1977). *The two-year college instructor today.* New York: Praeger.

Cohen, A.M., & Brawer, F.B. (1982). *The American community college.* San Francisco: Jossey-Bass.

Cohen, M.D., & March, J.G. (1982). *Leadership and ambiguity: The American college president.* New York: McGraw-Hill.

Coker, H.; Medley, D.M.; & Soar, R.S. (1980). How valid are expert opinions about effective teaching? *Phi Delta Kappan, 65* (3), 162.

Cross, K. Patricia (1976). *Accent on learning.* San Francisco: Jossey-Bass.

Dodds, H.W. (1962). *The academic president: Educator or caretaker?* New York: McGraw-Hill.

Easton, J.Q.; Forrest, E.P.; Goldman, R.E.; & Ludwig, L.M. (1984, May). *National Study of Effective Community College Teachers.* Unpublished manuscript, The City Colleges of Chicago.

Elbe, K.E. (1970). Project to improve college teaching. *Academe, 4,* 3–6.

Elbe, K.E. (1976). *The craft of teaching.* San Francisco: Jossey-Bass.

Ellner, C.L., & Barnes, C.P. (1983). *Studies of college teaching.* Lexington, MA: D.C. Heath.

Evans, M.G. (1970). The effects of supervisory behavior on the path-goal relationship. *Organizational Behavior and Human Performance*, 55, 277–298.

Farrar, E.; Neufeld, B.; & Miles, M.B. (1984). Effective school programs in high schools: Social promotion or movement by merit? *Phi Delta Kappan*, 65, (10), 701–706.

Feinberg, L. (1984, April 29). Remedial work seen as erosion of education. *The Washington Post*, pp. 1, A6, A7.

Forehand, G.A. (1968). On the interaction of persons and organizations. In R. Tagiuri & G. Litwin (Eds.), *Organizational climate: Exploration of a concept*. Boston: Division of Research, Harvard Business School.

Forehand, G., & Gilmer, B. (1964). Environmental variation in studies of organizational behavior. *Psychological Bulletin*, 22, 361–382.

Franklin, J.L. (1975a). Down the organization: Influence processes across levels of hierarchy. *Administrative Science Quarterly*, 20, 153–164.

Franklin, J.L. (1975b). Relations among four social-psychological aspects of organizations. *Administrative Science Quarterly*, 20, 422–433.

Fredericksen, N.; Jensen, O.; & Beaton, A.E. (1972). *Prediction of organizational behavior*. Elmsford, NJ: Pergamon.

Futrell, M.H. (1984). Towards excellence. *National Forum*, 44, 11–24.

Garcia, R., & Romanik, D. (Eds.) (1984). Volume II: Prescriptive education. In J. Preston (Ed.), *Miami-Dade Community College 1984 institutional self-study*. Miami: Miami-Dade Community College.

Garrison, R.H. (1967). *Junior college faculty issues and problems, a preliminary national appraisal*. Washington, DC: American Association of Junior Colleges. ED 012 177.

Gellerman, S.W. (1959). The company personality. *Management Review*, 48, 69–76.

Glassman, E. (1980). The teacher as leader. In K. Elbe (Ed.), *New directions for teaching and learning: Vol. 1 Improving teaching styles*. San Francisco: Jossey-Bass.

Good, T.L.; Biddle, B.J.; & Brophy, J.E. (1975). *Teachers make a difference*. New York: Holt, Rinehart, & Winston.

Gross, F.L., Jr. (1982). *Passages in teaching*. New York: Philosophical Library.

Guskey, T.R., & Easton, J.Q. (1983, April–June). The characteristic of very effective teachers in urban community colleges. *Community/Junior College Quarterly of Research and Practice*, 7 (3).

Harper, H.; Herrig, J.; Kelly, J.T.; & Schinoff, R.B. (1981, March). *Advisement and graduation information system*. Miami: Miami-Dade Community College.

Harper, H., & Schinoff, R.B. (1985). Miami-Dade Community College course sequencing pathways: A computerized course selection system. Unpublished paper, Miami-Dade Community College.

Hollinshead, B.S. (1936). The community college program. *Junior College Journal, 7,* 111–116.

Jones, A.P., & James, L.R. (1977). *Psychological and organizational climate: Dimensions and relationships.* Ft. Worth, TX: Institute of Behavioral Research.

Kamm, R.B. (1982). *Leadership for leadership: Number one priority for president and other university administrators.* Washington, DC: University Press of America.

Kelly, J.T. (1981, April). *Restructuring the academic program: A systems approach to educational reform at Miami-Dade Community College.* Miami: Miami-Dade Community College.

Klemp, G.O., Jr. (1977). Three factors of success. In D.W. Vermilye (Ed.), *Current issues in higher education.* San Francisco: Jossey-Bass.

Lange, A.G. (1927). *The Lange book: The collected writings of a great educational philosopher.* San Francisco: Trade Publishing Company.

Likert, R. (1961). *New patterns of management.* New York: McGraw-Hill.

Likert, R. (1967). *The human organization.* New York: McGraw-Hill.

Litwin, G.H.; Humphrey, J.W.; & Wilson, T.B. (1978). Organizational climate: A proven tool for improving performance. In W. Warner Burke (Ed.), *The cutting edge: Current theory and practice in organizational development.* La Jolla, CA: University Associates, Inc.

Litwin, G.H., & Stringer, R. (1966, March). The influence of organizational climate on human motivation. Paper presented at the Conference on Organizational Climate, Foundation for Research on Human Behavior, Ann Arbor, MI.

Litwin, G.H., & Stringer, R. (1968). *Motivation and organizational climate.* Cambridge, MA: Harvard University Press.

Losak, J. (1983). Diversity in the American public two-year college. (Report No. 83–26). Miami: Miami-Dade Community College Office of Institutional Research.

Losak, J. (1983, May). *Status of the impacts of the reforms which have been initiated at Miami-Dade during the past five years.* (Research Report No. 83–13). Miami: Miami-Dade Community College.

Losak, J. (1984a, February). *Relating grade point average at Miami-Dade to subsequent student performance on the College Level Academic Skills Test (CLAST).* (Research Report No. 84–03). Miami: Miami-Dade Community College.

Losak, J. (1984b, April). *Success on the CLAST for those students who enter the college academically underprepared.* (Research Report No. 84-04). Miami: Miami-Dade Community College.

Losak, J. (1984c, December). *Academic progress of students at Miami-Dade who were initially not eligible to enroll in the state-university system.* (Research Report No. 84-30). Miami: Miami-Dade Community College.

Losak, J., & Morris, C. (1982, November). *Retention, graduation, and academic progress related to academic skills.* (Research Report No. 82-36). Miami: Miami-Dade Community College.

Losak, J., & Morris, C. (1983a, July). *Impact of the standards of academic progress on student achievement and persistence at Miami-Dade Community College.* (Research Report No. 83-23). Miami: Miami-Dade Community College.

Losak, J., & Morris, C. (1983b, December). *Effect of student self-selection into remedial classes.* (Research Report No. 83-23). Miami: Miami-Dade Community College.

Lukenbill, J.D., & McCabe, R.H. (1978). *General education in a changing society.* Dubuque, IA: Kendall/Hunt.

McCabe, R.H. (1982). Quality and the open-door community college. *Current Issues in Higher Education: Underprepared learners, 1.* Washington, DC: American Association of Higher Education.

McCabe, R.H. (1981, March). *The educational reform at Miami-Dade Community College is resulting in improved student performance.* Miami: Miami-Dade Community College.

McCabe, R.H. (1983a). *Information skills for the information age.* Miami: Miami-Dade Community College.

McCabe, R.H. (1983b). *A status report on the comprehensive educational reform of Miami-Dade Community College.* Miami: Miami-Dade Community College.

McCabe, R.H. (1984a, November). *The reform of the educational program at Miami-Dade Community College.* Miami: Miami-Dade Community College.

McCabe, R.H. (1984b, November). *Why Miami-Dade Community College is reforming the educational system.* Miami: Miami-Dade Community College.

McCabe, R.H. (in press). Equity and quality in college education: An essential American priority. In J.B. Bennett & J.W. Peltason (Eds.), *Contemporary issues in higher education.* New York: American Council on Education/Macmillan.

McCabe, R.H., & Kelly, T. (1983). Learner reward case study: Miami-Dade Community College. In J.E. Roueche & G.A. Baker, *Beacons* for change: An innovative outcome model for community colleges. The American College Testing Program.

McCabe, R.H., & Skidmore, S.G. (1983, September). Miami-Dade: Results justify reforms. *Community and Junior College Journal, 54,* (1), 26–29.

McClelland, D. (1978). *Guide to behavioral interviewing.* Boston: McBer.

McKeachie, W.J. (1978). *Teaching tips* (7th ed.). Lexington, MA: D.C. Heath.

Medley, D. (1979). The effectiveness of teachers. In P. Peterson & H.J. Walberg (Eds.), *Research on teaching: Concepts, findings and implications.* Berkeley: McCutchan.

Medsker, L.L. (1960). *The junior college: Progress and prospect.* New York: McGraw-Hill.

Miller, R.I. (1972). *Evaluating faculty performance.* San Francisco: Jossey-Bass.

Miller, R.I. (1974). *Developing programs for faculty evaluation.* San Francisco: Jossey-Bass.

Moos, R. (1973). Conceptualization of human environments. *American Psychologist, 28,* 652–665.

Morris, C. (1983, April). *Equal access/equal opportunity research at Miami-Dade Community College: Fall 1976–77 through fall 1981–82 cohorts.* (Research Report No. 83–09). Miami: Miami-Dade Community College.

Mullin, P.L.M. (1985). A study of leadership competencies found to be associated with positive organization climate and institutional efficacy at Miami-Dade Community College. Unpublished doctoral dissertation, The University of Texas at Austin, Austin, TX.

Murphy, J.F.; Weil, M.; Hallinger, P.; & Mitman, A. (1982). Academic press: Translating high expectations into school policies and classroom practices. *Educational Leadership, 40* (3), 22–26.

National Institute of Education. (1984, October). *Involvement in learning: Realizing the potential of American higher education.* Washington, DC: U.S. Government Printing Office.

No ivy on the walls: A history of Miami-Dade Community College. (1982). Miami: Miami-Dade Community College.

Office of Institutional Research (1985, January). *1984 Factbook: Miami-Dade Community College.* Miami: Miami-Dade Community College.

Ossip, B.A. (Ed.). (1984). Volume IV: Student information and performance standards. In J. Preston (Ed.), *Miami-Dade Community College 1984 institutional self-study.* Miami: Miami-Dade Community College.

Payne, R.L., & Pugh, D. (1976). Organizational structure and climate. In M.D. Dunnete (Ed.), *Handbook of industrial and organizational psychology*. Chicago: Rand McNally.

Popham, W.J. (1973). *Evaluating instruction*. Englewood Cliffs, NJ: Prentice-Hall.

Preston, J. (Ed.). (1984). *Miami-Dade Community College 1984 institutional self-study: Vol. 1, Summary and recommendations*. Miami: Miami-Dade Community College.

Ritchie, J.B., & Thompson, P. (1976). *Organization and people: Readings, cases, and exercises in organizational behavior*. St. Paul: West.

Roberts, R. (Ed.). (1984). Volume III: Academic policies and curriculum reforms. In J. Preston (Ed.), *Miami-Dade Community College 1984 institutional self-study*. Miami: Miami-Dade Community College.

Robertson, P.F., & Thomas, S.C. (1981, May). *Emphasis on excellence*. Miami: Miami-Dade Community College.

Rockefeller Brothers Fund (1958). *The pursuit of excellence*. (Special Studies Report 5). New York: Doubleday.

Rothman, J. (1974). *Planning and organizing for social change*. New York: Columbia University Press.

Roueche, J.E. (1982, May). The need for excellence in college teaching. In *Promoting great teaching: A staff development imperative*, Proceedings of the National Institute on Staff Development, Austin, TX: The University of Texas. ERIC ED 221 150.

Roueche, J.E.; Baker, G.A., III; Mullin, P.L.; & Omaha Boy, N.H. (in press). *Profiles in teaching excellence: America's best schools*. Arlington, VA: American Association of School Administrators.

Schein, E.H. (1983). The role of the founder in creating organizational culture. *Organizational Dynamics, 12* (1), 13–28.

Schein, E.H. (1985). *Organizational culture and leadership: A dynamic view*. San Francisco: Jossey-Bass.

Schneider, B. (1975). Organizational climates: An essay. *Personnel Psychology, 28*, 447–479.

Schneider, B., & Bartlett, C.J. (1968). Individual differences and organizational climate, I: The research plan and questionnaire development. *Personnel Psychology, 21*, 323–334.

Schneider, B., & Bartlett, C.J. (1970). Measurement of organizational climate by the multi-trait, multi-rater matrix. *Personnel Psychology, 28*, 447–479.

Schneider, B., & Snyder, R.A. (1975). Some relationships between job satisfaction and organizational climate. *Journal of Applied Psychology, 60*, 318–328.

Schneider, C.; Klemp, G.O., Jr.; & Kastendiek, S. (1981). *The balancing act: Competencies of effective teachers and mentors in degree programs for adults.* Chicago: University of Chicago and Boston: McBer.

Sergiovanni, T.J. (1984). Leadership and excellence in schooling. *Educational Leadership, 41* (5), 6–13.

Skidmore, S.G. (1983). *Education for the real world: Miami-Dade Community College.* Miami: Miami-Dade Community College.

Stallings, J. (1981). *What research has to say to administrators of secondary schools about effective teaching and staff development.* ERIC ED 209 748.

Steers, R.M. (1977). *Organizational effectiveness: A behavioral view.* Santa Monica, CA: Goodyear.

Stokes, R. (1981, October). *Revitalizing the physical education requirement: Health analysis and improvement.* Miami: Miami-Dade Community College.

Taylor, J.C., & Bowers, D. (1972). *Survey of organizations: A machine scored standardized instrument.* Ann Arbor: University of Michigan, Institute for Social Research.

Troisi, N.F. *Effective teaching and student achievement.* Reston, VA: National Association of Secondary School Principals. ERIC ED 231 067.

Tyler, R.W. (1958). The evaluation of teaching. In R.M. Cooper (Ed.), *The two ends of the log.* Minneapolis: University of Minnesota Press.

Vaughan, G.B., & Associates (1983). *Issues for community college leaders in a new era.* San Francisco: Jossey-Bass.

Ware, B.A. (1978, January). What rewards do students want? *Phi Delta Kappan, 59* (5), 356.

Webb, W.B., & Nolan, C.Y. (1955). Student, supervisor, and self-ratings of instructional proficiency. *The Journal of Educational Psychology, 46,* 42–46.

Wilson, J.D. (1981). *Student learning in higher education.* New York: John Wiley & Sons.

Wilson, R.C.; Gaff, J.G.; Dienst, E.R.; Wood, L.; & Bavry, J.L. (1975). *College professors and their impact on students.* New York: John Wiley & Sons.

Wotruba, T.R., & Wright, P.L. (1975). How to develop a teacher-rating instrument: A research approach. *Journal of Higher Education, 46* (6), 653–663.

Zwerling, L.S. *Second best: The crisis of the community college.* New York: McGraw-Hill.

ABOUT THE AUTHORS

John E. Roueche is Professor of Educational Administration and Director of the Community College Leadership Program at The University of Texas at Austin. He is the author of more than 100 books, monographs, and articles on educational leadership and teaching effectiveness. In 1982, he received The University of Texas Teaching Excellence Award. Two of his books, *Overcoming Learning Problems*, 1977, and *College Responses to Low-Achieving Students*, 1984 (with George A. Baker and Suanne D. Roueche) earned him the Council of Universities and Colleges Outstanding Research Publication Awards. He also received the 1984 Distinguished Research Award from the National Association of Developmental Education, the 1985 University of Texas Outstanding Researcher Award, and most recently, the 1986 National Leadership Award from the American Association of Community and Junior Colleges.

In great demand as a conference and convention keynote speaker, Roueche has spoken to more than 1,100 college, university, and public school faculties since 1970.

As Project Director of the National Institute for Staff and Organizational Development, Roueche has spearheaded the establishment of a national network of more than 460 colleges and universities committed to the improvement of teaching effectiveness and to the professional growth and development of teachers and administrators. In 1980 a national study at Florida State University identified him as the outstanding living author in the field of community college education.

George A. Baker III is Associate Professor of Educational Administration at The University of Texas at Austin, where he was selected as the 1983 recipient of The University's Teaching Excellence Award. A former member of the White House staff under President Lyndon Johnson, Baker taught on the faculties of the U.S. Naval War College, The University of Virginia, and Furman University. He has also served as Vice President for Academic Affairs at Greenville Technical College (S.C.) and as the founding director of the National Institute for Staff and Organizational Development (NISOD), at The University of Texas at Austin.

A prolific researcher, writer, and public speaker, Baker was honored in 1984 by the Council of Universities and Colleges for the results of his national study (with Roueche and Roueche) of college programs for underprepared students. In 1984, he was also selected to teach the first undergraduate honors course in the College of Education at The University of Texas at Austin.

Patricia L. Meyer Mullin is currently Associate Dean at Fort Steilacoom Community College, Tacoma, Washington. She has had extensive teaching experience in both high school and junior high school followed by faculty experience at The University of Iowa. She served on the faculty of Lane Community College (Oregon) for a number of years and later taught at The University of Oregon in Eugene. Prior to her work at The University of Texas at Austin, she taught in high schools in Alexandria, Egypt, and then later at the Saudi Arabian International School in Dhahran, Saudi Arabia. She completed her Ph.D. in educational administration in August 1985.

Nancy Hess Omaha Boy is Dean at Wenatchee Valley College, Omak, Washington. She joined the research staff at The University of Texas after having served as Provost of the McConnell Air Force Base Campus with Butler County Community College (Kansas). She also served as Professor and Acting Chair in the Department of Education at Sinte Gleska College, South Dakota, and earlier directed educational programs for the Wisconsin Winnebago Tribe. She has teaching experience abroad and has extensive background in the development of programs and courses for native American populations in Wisconsin and South Dakota.

INDEX

PROPER NAMES AND INSTITUTIONS